The British Josiah

"Edward VI... The Most Godly King of England"

(Quotation from John Knox)

The King History Forgot

He was spoken of as an "angel in a human body" by those who knew him best. His godly life-style and his delight in the Scriptures from the time he was a child created the impression that he was indeed a superior person. He was referred to as "the British Josiah" during his lifetime and long after. Like the Bible King Josiah, "while he was yet young, he began to seek the God of David his father." Both—Josiah the king of Judah and the "British Josiah"— in their early years moved against the prevailing idolatry.

Sir John Cheke, a godly man with superb credentials was tutor and personal friend for most of his life. Men of great learning and dedication, including Cranmer, Ridley and Latimer loved the young prince and trained him in the deep things of God.

Three swords, emblematic of his three kingdoms, were brought to be carried in the coronation procession. The king said, "there was one yet wanting." When asked what it was, he answered with conviction, "the Bible."

Armed with the facts of history and imbued with the power-light of the holy Scriptures, the king, when scarcely twelve years of age, wrote his great discourse titled "Against the Primacy of the Pope." This was a landmark achievement for the enlightenment of the English people who for centuries lived in spiritual darkness. One hundred thirty-three years later, the treatise resurfaced to declare once again Christ's supremacy over the church.

Though young in years the king witnessed faithfully to his sisters and friends.

The royal Reformer did not neglect the poor in his own city. He gave generously of his properties under the guidance of Bishop Ridley, the Mayor of London and his advisors.

The use of poison to end his life cannot be ruled out, but like Enoch of old, King Edward VI "walked with God, and was not for God took him" (Gen. 5:24).

The British Josiah

"Edward VI... the Most Godly King of England"

N.A. Woychuk, M. A., Th. D.

Author, "Messiah, A New Look at the Composer, the
Music and the Message," "Building Gold," etc.

General Index on the biography
by Gladys Teague

Cover by Jeffery Terpstra

SMF PRESS
P.O. Box 411551
St. Louis, MO 63141

Library of Congress Catalog card number: 2001_131849

ISBN 1-880960-45-1

Dedication

With all the love God has put in my heart this book is respectfully dedicated to all sincere Catholics—to those who are born again by faith in Jesus Christ alone—and to those who are earnestly seeking the way of salvation. The author of this book was born into a devout Catholic family and by memorizing Bible verses to impress a school master he saw the truth of the Gospel and was born again by simple faith in Jesus Christ as Savior.

It is no mischance that sincere and educated people—Catholic and Protestant alike—miss the truth of salvation revealed in the Bible. The reason for this is due to the fact that the "god of this world" (Satan) blinds them (2 Corinthians 4:3,4) so that they stumble at the truth. They need only to believe the word of God, receive the Lord Jesus Christ as Savior and "pass from death unto life" (John 5:24). Salvation comes as a gift from God. "For by grace are you saved through faith; and that not of yourselves: it is the gift of God: not of works, lest any man should boast" (Eph. 2:8, 9).

HOUSE OF TUDOR

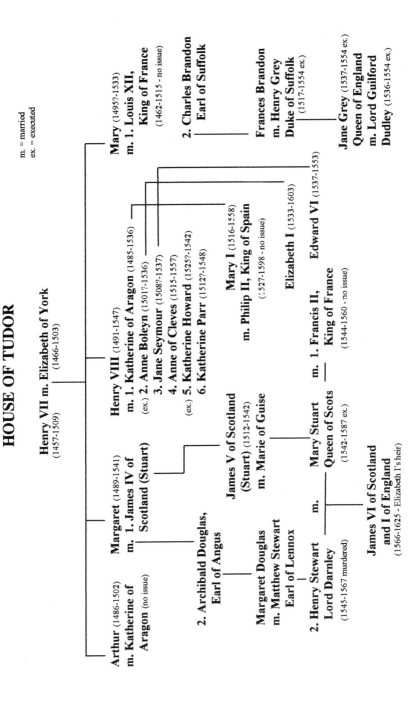

m. = married
ex. = executed

Henry VII m. Elizabeth of York
(1457-1509)   (1466-1503)

Arthur (1486-1502)
m. **Katherine of Aragon** (no issue)

Margaret (1489-1541)
m. 1. **James IV of Scotland (Stuart)**

2. **Archibald Douglas, Earl of Angus**

Margaret Douglas
m. **Matthew Stewart Earl of Lennox**

James V of Scotland (Stuart) (1512-1542)
m. **Marie of Guise**

2. **Henry Stewart Lord Darnley**
(1545-1567 murdered)

Mary Stuart Queen of Scots
(1542-1587 ex.)

m. 1. **Francis II, King of France**
(1544-1560 - no issue)

m.

James VI of Scotland and I of England
(1566-1625 - Elizabeth I's heir)

Henry VIII (1491-1547)
m. 1. **Katherine of Aragon** (1485-1536)
(ex.) 2. **Anne Boleyn** (1501?-1536)
3. **Jane Seymour** (1508?-1537)
4. **Anne of Cleves** (1515-1557)
(ex.) 5. **Katherine Howard** (1525?-1542)
6. **Katherine Parr** (1512?-1548)

Mary I (1516-1558)
m. **Philip II, King of Spain**
(1527-1598 - no issue)

Elizabeth I (1533-1603)

Edward VI (1537-1553)

Mary (1495?-1533)
m. 1. **Louis XII, King of France**
(1462-1515 - no issue)

2. **Charles Brandon Earl of Suffolk**

Frances Brandon
m. **Henry Grey Duke of Suffolk**
(1517-1554 ex.)

Jane Grey (1537-1554 ex.)
Queen of England
m. **Lord Guilford Dudley** (1536-1554 ex.)

vi

Table of Contents

The Royal Light Among the Reformers

William Tyndale was returning to England from the continent when he was apprehended by the Roman Catholic zealots and was executed near Brussels in 1536. Before he was burned he prayed, "Lord, open the king of England's eyes." The following year a boy was born to Henry VIII and his wife *Jane Seymour*. He became king of England—Edward VI—at the age of nine.

The strong Christian testimony and writings of Edward were treasures of immeasurable value in building the foundations of the Protestant Reformation, where the holy Scriptures were regarded as the paramount guide for all spiritual matters in faith and practice. Unfortunately the writings of King Edward VI have been set aside and biographers of this great

1

monarch have said very little about them or totally disregarded them. On that account, an important chapter in the history of the Reformation has been neglected.

I became aware of this while reading a letter, dated August 3, 1553, from *John Calvin* in Geneva to *Henry Bullinger* in Zurich. I found a footnote with that letter which immediately captured my full attention. These are the words: "That most pious king of England departed to the Lord on the 6th of July—and he departed very happily indeed with a holy confession. *The book which I here send you was written by him and published in the month of May. You will see from it how great a treasure the Church of Christ has lost.*" [1]

Immediately, I made a search for this book in the archives of Berne and Zurich, Switzerland, but without any success. After numerous communications, it was located in London, and is now in my possession. The book contains Edward's remarkable treatise, *Against the Primacy of the Pope* and some choice particulars concerning Edward's God-directed life.

He grew up "as a tender plant" and his spiritual stature began to be known at his coronation on February 28, 1547, following the death of his father the month before.

Three swords, emblematic of his three kingdoms,

[1] G. C. Gorham, *Gleanings of a Few Scattered Ears, During the Period of the Reformation in England,* Bell and Daldy, London.

were brought to be carried in the procession. The king saw them and said, "There was one yet wanting." When asked what it was, he answered with conviction, "the Bible," adding further, "That book is the sword of the Spirit, and is to be preferred before these swords . . . .Without that sword we are nothing, we can do nothing, we have not power. From the Bible we are what we are this day." [2]

Such words must have cast a holy silence upon all who heard them. Search all of English history and you will not find anything spoken by any English monarch that is even faintly comparable.

Obviously, he was a "planting of the Lord," raised up for such a time in a land that was kept in darkness by the blind religious leaders.

Edward's chief tutor was *Sir John Cheke,* and he was nurtured and guided by the great reformers, including *Thomas Cranmer, Hugh Latimer,* and *Nicholas Ridley.* He was also influenced by the outstanding reformers from abroad, including *Martin Bucer, Peter Martyr, John Calvin* and *John Knox.*

He delighted in the holy Scriptures and grew like a tree planted by the rivers of water. His walk and his words soon earned him the title—"The British Josiah."

Of the Bible Josiah it is written, "And he did that which was right in the sight of the Lord, and walked

[2] *Writings of Edward the Sixth,* The Religious Tract Society, London, 1831.

3

in the ways of David his father, and declined neither to the right hand, nor to the left"(2 Chron. 34:2).

This boy had the mark of God on him and the world would soon witness the results.

Edward's superb treatise titled, *Against the Primacy of the Pope* is a true and powerful message for all time, although biographers generally disregard this great work of the young king or say very little concerning it.

We are aware of the fact that this message is loaded with spiritual dynamite. Perhaps, in the providence of God, it was timed to ignite and explode at such a time as this when many religious leaders—worldwide—are befuddled concerning the supreme authority of the Scriptures and are careless in their statements and associations. "Can two walk together, except they be agreed?" (Amos 3:3). Those who compromise the Word of God soon find themselves in fellowship with unbelievers.

We seek the guidance of the Holy Spirit and welcome your prayers, that this powerful message will awaken our generation to an understanding of the true gospel and the proclaiming of it without compromise.

During Edward VI's reign, great reforms were initiated and the moral corruption began to be checked. In the six short years of his reign, the nation "had been revolutionized. The foundations for the enlargement of true Christianity in England were laid in the encouragement given to the people to read, mark, learn and inwardly digest the word of God." [3] They were taught that the Gospel has God for its author, salvation for its end, and truth, without any admixture of error, for its matter. He sought to instruct his sister Mary, who scornfully rejected his counsel. He did, however, help his sister Elizabeth, who followed Queen Mary, as the English monarch in whose reign Protestantism was resumed and more fully established in England.

His untimely death, when he was three months short of being 16 years of age, was deeply mourned and lamented by all believers in England and among many on the continent. *John Calvin*, second only to *Luther* in the Protestant Reformation, said in a letter to *Farell*, dated August 7, 1553, "Most truly do you say, that the land has been deprived of an incomparable treasure. Indeed, I consider that, by the death of one youth, the whole nation has been bereaved of the best of fathers." *John Knox*, the Scottish reformer, described him as "that most godly and virtuous king that has ever been known to have reigned in England."

February 1, 2001   —N. A. Woychuk

[3] *A Short History of the Reformation*, Protestant Truth Society, London.

5

In Memory of Edward *VI*

O Lord how various are the ways
  How infinite the skill,
Wherewith Thou formest to Thy praise
  The creatures of Thy will.

To babes and sucklings 'tis Thy joy
  Heaven's secret to impart,
And all Thy wisdom to employ
  Upon the obedient heart.

Then oft a converse work as well
  Is by Thy counsels wrought,
And reason's masters own Thy spell,
  To childlike reverence brought.

In either case with love and awe
  The self-same hands we greet;
The lowliest to Thy heart they draw,
  The loftiest to Thy feet.

'Tis Thine to bid the outcast find
  His God within his breast,
And Thine to win an Edward's mind
  At Calvary's cross to rest.

—Bishop Handley C. G. Moule

(adapted)

❧ 1 ❧

William Tyndale's Last Prayer

The Year was 1536.

Deep spiritual darkness lay across England and the continent.

The crime was truth! And a man of God was condemned to be burned.

But the flames had no mercy for they knew not the innocence of their victim, *William Tyndale*. But before the hot flames did their utmost to destroy the God-fearing man—in those final moments—he prayed fervently, but the prayer was not for himself, but for all the people who lived in darkness. This was the agonizing prayer for their enlightenment, and before he was strangled and burned he cried out with "fervent zeal and a loud voice," *"Lord! open the king of England's eyes."* [1]

John Wicliffe (1329-1384), "The Morning Star

[1] William Byron Forbush, editor, *Foxe's Book of Martyrs*, John C. Winston Co., Philadelphia, 1926.

of the Reformation," as he came to be known, risked his life daily in translating the Scriptures and having them written out and distributed among the people. The large extent of Wicliffe's work in laying the foundation for the Reformation among the people of England cannot be overstated. While he taught at Oxford, people from the continent came under the influence of his clear Bible teaching. They carried the message to their people back home, and one of the recipients of the true Gospel was *John Huss* (1373-1415) of Bohemia, who was among the first to suffer martyrdom for the faith.

The Spirit of God stirred in the heart of William Tyndale (1494-1536) with the same conviction regarding the urgent need of circulating the Scriptures among the people. "He perceived that it was not possible to establish the lay people in the truth, except the Scriptures were so plainly laid before their eyes in their mother tongue that they might see the meaning of the text; or else, whatsoever truth should be taught them, the enemies of the truth would quench it." [2]

Whereas Wicliffe translated from the Latin, Tyndale did his translation work from the Greek in which the original text was first written. God enabled Tyndale to translate the Scriptures in the manner desired. In order to facilitate the printing of the Scriptures, Tyndale went to Germany, and soon the

[2] Ibid.

8

printed portions of the Scriptures were pouring into London.

This aroused the antipathy of the Roman Catholic authorities, who held total sovereignty over most of the nations of the continent of Europe as well as England. They did not want the people to read the word of God because it set them "free" (Jn. 1:32) and brought the desire to shake off the yoke of Rome. They caught up with Tyndale in Belgium at Antwerp when he was making an effort to return to England. His treacherous foes struck, arrested him and thrust him into prison near Brussels, Belgium, where a year later he was strangled and burned at the stake in 1536. It was at his execution that he called upon God to open the spiritual understanding of the king, so that he would lead the people to know and believe the Gospel of Jesus Christ, the one and only Savior.

The following year, on October 12, 1537, a child was born to *King Henry VIII* and *Jane Seymour* at two o'clock in the morning at Hampton Court Palace. By daylight the news was out all over London, and the city erupted in rapturous expressions of joy and delight. By nightfall, bonfires blazed throughout the nation with the joyous message that the House of Tudor now had a living male heir.

Historians appear to be in agreement that of his several wives, Jane Seymour is the only woman King Henry VIII really loved. The queen died twelve days after giving birth to the boy who became King Edward VI nine years later.

Although the country grieved over the death of the queen, the birth of a prince, which had long been desired, brought great joy to all.

Those who came in contact with the child were at once attracted to him, and their sympathy, affection and attention were unbounded. He had a thin body, very much a duplicate of his beautiful mother with her "fair hair, pointed chin, and rather tight lips." His smiles, his beauty and loving mannerisms only increased the admiration of the people. "His eyes," said one observer, "seemed to have a starry liveliness and lustre."

At long last England had a monarch that would bring them out of darkness using the light of the Scriptures. Some of the Christians may have prayed that this would be the king whose eyes would be opened by God to accept the Scriptures as God's complete revelation to sinful men. As the child grew and began his witness for the Lord, there was no question in the minds of the *enlightened* people but that Edward VI was indeed the *king whose eyes God opened* in answer to Tyndale's prayer.

~2~

The Influence of Edward's Father King Henry VIII

King Henry the Eighth died on January 28, 1547, leaving his kingdom to his nine-year-old son, Edward. In his last will, dated December 30, 1546, Henry named sixteen executors, who were also to form his son's Privy Council and have the government of his son and his realms and of all public and private affairs until Edward reached the age of eighteen.

Henry the Eighth was something of an enigma. He broke with the Pope of Rome, sanctioned the destruction of monastic buildings, made Cranmer and Ridley bishops, and permitted the Bible to be circulated throughout his realm, yet Henry distinctly maintained Roman Catholicism in its most papal form of doctrine.

There is no desire here to defend him, for in many

ways he was a wicked man. Yet it is an indisputable fact that during Henry's reign the power of Romanism in England began to crumble. God has often done a great and good work with inferior tools.

We see the king's influence in the right direction in three or four situations.

In his last and best speech before the House of Lords he turned their minds to the word of God. Based on 1 Corinthians chapter 13, he spoke on "charity." He reminded them that by his license they were permitted to have and to read the holy Scriptures in their mother tongue, but only to inform their consciences and for the instruction of their families, not to feed disputation and divide the realm by brawling dissensions. "I am sorry to know," the king said, "how unreverently that most precious jewel, the Word of God, is disputed, rhymed, sung and jangled in every alehouse and tavern, contrary to the true meaning and doctrine of the same." [1]

There runs through the fiber of his speech almost a desperate plea that his realm gently embrace Protestantism, in which the Word of God was the chief mainspring.

The choice of instructors that Henry made for his young son, the next king of England, unmistakably points towards the faith taught by Protestants. *Dr. Richard Cox*, whose firm persuasion was that

---

[1] W. K. Jordan, *Edward VI: The Young King,* Harvard University Press, Cambridge, MA., 1968.

of a moderate Protestant, was chosen to become Edward's almoner and tutor and was to be completely in charge of the child's education. As close assistant, the king chose *Sir John Cheke*, of Cambridge. These two men, both Protestant in their convictions, were, in the providence of God, given the task of bringing up the prince in learning of tongues, of the Scripture, of philosophy and all liberal sciences. Such appointments made the true hearts of England rejoice.

The king's influence for Protestantism may also be seen in the tacit approval which he gave to the queen—*Katherine Parr*—to publish the influential tracts which went out under her name. (The tracts were a means of instruction and exerted a great influence for the Protestant cause.) She was sympathetic with such undoubted Protestants as *Miles Coverdale*, the Bible translator and *Nicholas Udall*.

Despite Henry's rigid Catholicism, it is well to note that he had in considerable measure prepared his realm to embrace Protestantism in the reign of his son, Edward VI.

It was January 27th, 1547 and physicians were in attendance at the king's bedchamber. The king, Henry VIII, was sinking rapidly. About eleven o'clock *Sir Anthony Denny* approached the bedside, and said: "In man's judgment, Your Majesty is not like to live. I beseech Your Majesty to prepare yourself for death, and to consider the sins of your life past." There was a pause. Then Henry replied calmly, "The mercy of Christ is able to pardon me all my sins, though they were greater than they be."

When asked if he desired to confer with any learned man, the king asked for Cranmer. The man of God arrived at midnight. By then Henry was speechless, but he stretched out his hand to Cranmer, who held it fast and who pleaded with Henry to give him some sign that he was trusting Jesus Christ as Savior. The king gripped Cranmer's hand tightly. As his hold relaxed, he sank into unconsciousness. This could be another case of salvation comparable to that of the thief on the cross.

Only God knows.

At two o'clock in the morning of January 28th, 1547, Edward Tudor became king of England.

Before King Henry died—perhaps having some premonition of his approaching decease—he distributed impressive quantities of jewelry to his family. For Edward, the heir apparent, were reserved the most magnificent items of all—including, as Edward wrote his appreciation to his father " . . . chains, rings, jewelled buttons, neck chains and breast pins, and necklaces, garments and many other things, in which your fatherly affection towards me is conspicuous," and even at age of nine, Edward reasoned correctly, "For if you did not love me, you would not give me these fine gifts of jewelry." As was the custom, none of Henry's children attended the funeral.

Spiritual Darkness Covered the Land

Prior to the reign of Henry VIII, spiritual darkness prevailed throughout the land. The word of God had vanished into a mysterious obscurity through the design of the religious leaders in each generation. Several attempts had been made to translate or paraphrase various portions of the Bible. The venerable *Bede* (673-738) translated the Lord's prayer and the Gospel of John into Saxon; the learned men at the court of *King Alfred the Great* (849-899) translated the four Gospels; *Elfric*, in the reign of *Ethelred* (1295-1349), translated some books of the Old Testament; an Anglo-Norman priest paraphrased the Gospels and Acts. *Richard Rolle* (1329-1384), "the hermit of Hampole" produced a version of the Psalms, the Gospels and the Epistles. But all these efforts of godly men were promptly hidden, like theological curiosities, in the libraries of the convents and monasteries.

In Wicliffe's time, as in previous generations, the reading of the Bible was considered to be injurious to the laity and the small portions that were made available were intended for the clergy and the educated class.

While the papal world was in commotion, John

Wicliffe, (1329-1384) with his Latin Vulgate Bible before him at the quiet rectory of Lutterworth, undertook the translation of the whole Bible into the English tongue. The great work was completed in 1382. Here are four verses from John 14, as contained in that version:

"Be not youre herete afraid, ne drede it; ye blieuen in God, and bileue ye in me. In the hous of my fadir ben many dwellyngis; if ony thing lesse, Y hadde seid to you, for y go to make redi to yo a place. And if Y go, and make redi to you a place eftsoones Y come, and Y schal take you to my silf, that where I am, ye be. And whidur I go, ye witen, and ye witen the weie."

Now the Bible was available in the language of the people and Wicliffe and his helpers begged the friars strolling over the country, preaching the legends of the saints and the history of the Trojan war, to take the Bible and preach the word of God to the people.

Some did and where the Gospel was proclaimed there was light and life; soon, however, the copies of the Bible were restricted to the convents and monasteries, as were the previous portions. And spiritual darkness continued to cover the land.

Men and women needed relief. They had sorrow, sickness and death, just like we do. Where could they turn? There was no one to tell them about the love of God and the mediation of Christ. They were not told the glad tidings of free, full and complete salvation, justification by faith and growth in holiness through the word of God and the work of the Holy Spirit.

The people could only turn to the priests, who knew nothing themselves and could teach nothing to others. "The blind lead the blind, both shall fall into the ditch" (Matt. 15:14). In short, the religion in those days was little better than "an organized system of Virgin Mary worship, saint worship, image worship, relic worship, pilgrimages, almsgivings, formalism, ceremonialism, processions, prostrations, bowings, crossings, fastings, confessions, absolutions, masses, penances, and blind obedience to the priests." [2] The only practical result was that the priests took the people's money, and the people flattered themselves that the more they gave to the priests, the more likelihood there was of their going to heaven.

At the Abbey of Hales, in Gloucestershire, a vial was shown by the priests to those who offered alms. They were told by the priests that the vial contained the blood of Christ. On examination in the time of King Henry the Eighth, this notable vial was found to contain nothing more and nothing less that the blood of a duck, which was renewed every week.

[2] *Writings of Edward the Sixth,* The Religious Tract Society, London, 1831.

When *John Hooper* became bishop of Gloucester in 1551, he found that out of 311 clergy in his diocese, 168 were unable to repeat the Ten Commandments; 31 of the 168 could not state in what part of the Bible they were to be found. Forty could not tell where the Lord's prayer was written, and 31 of the 40 were ignorant as to who was the author of the Lord's prayer.

~3~

The Training of Edward

It is cheap work to find fault in the character of some of the agents whom God was pleased to use in bringing about the glorious Reformation in the Christianity of England. Henry the Eighth was far from the finest among men, but we see him rising to the top when it comes to the training of his children.

Until the age of six Edward lived "among the women," as he later put it,[1] but, judging from his remarkable spiritual progress they must have been godly women. Then he was committed to the charge of able Christian tutors and instructors. *Sir Anthony Cook*, who believed the Gospel and whose own children were being trained in the word of God, was his chief instructor at the beginning.

---

[1] W. K. Jordan, editor, *The Chronicle and Political Papers of King Edward VI,* Cornell University Press, 1966.

Dr. Richard Cox, became Edward's almoner and tutor when Edward was about six years of age. Edward was deeply concerned that his father should capture Boulogne from France, England's ancient enemy. With that in mind Dr. Cox based his teaching on the pretense that Edward first besieged and then assaulted the duller parts of learning. The eight parts of speech were the defenders; as soon as they became the "subjects and servants" of the prince, he must now tear down the outworks of the Latin nouns and verbs.

At first Edward took to this game with considerable enthusiasm. He conquered the outposts of grammar very well. He was then primed to go after the new territory, including Latin, Cato and Aesop. Dr. Cox insisted on daily learning by heart some of Solomon's Proverbs. This became irksome and the royal pupil wearied of the Jewish monarch's admonitions about discipline, the Commandments and filial obedience. Dr. Cox resorted to his earlier tactics and told his pupil that he was faced with a great enemy, "Captain Will," who must be defeated before any further progress could be made.

Still the pupil remained unmoved. The military approach had lost its charm. Dr. Cox tried coaxing and threatening, but Edward stood aloof. Although Cox did not want to resort to the old-fashioned way, forthwith the occasion arose and Dr. Cox hit Edward very hard—whether he used a rod or the flat of his hand we are not told. It was a shock to the pupil and a definite victory for the tutor. Dr. Cox completed his task with a deepening of love for his pupil and pride in all of his accomplishments.

In January 1546, Cox informed Archbishop Cranmer that the young prince had learned almost four books of Cato, some of *Aesop's Fables*, many Bible texts and Vives' *Satellitium*. Edward also read the standard texts of the times: Erasmus's *Colloquies*, Cicero, Pliny the Younger, Herodotus, Plutarch and Thucydides.

Edward began to learn French in 1546, and by December he had advanced sufficiently to write a letter in French to his sister Elizabeth. He was also learning Spanish and Italian.

Dr. Cox had to leave his pupil when he was appointed dean of Christ Church College and Chancellor of Oxford University.

When it was suggested to the boy that he write his absent tutor a letter, he did so promptly. Not desiring to spend much time on it, he slyly wrote in Latin, and cleverly excused his shortcoming with a classical quotation:

> "I send to you a short letter, my dearest almoner, because I know short letters are to you as acceptable as long ones. For I am well aware that you have read Cato's first book, twentieth verse, 'When a poor friend gives you a little present, accept it kindly,

and remember to praise it amply.' Though my letter is short, it wanteth not good will. I pray God to preserve you in safety and in health."[2]

After Dr. Cox left, *Sir John Cheke*, the learned professor of Greek at Cambridge was appointed tutor to the prince. Cheke fulfilled the role of father, brother, uncle and friend. Cheke always provided a welcome atmosphere for the young orphaned prince. He was a warm and witty tutor, and in a time when the schoolmaster was known to be stern, this was unusual. He planned it so that Edward would have classmates; therefore, eight or ten other children of similar age were brought together to form a Palace school, giving the young prince some classmates with whom to compete athletically and academically.

Warm-hearted, sensitive and witty, Cheke infected his pupils with an enthusiasm that made each session a special event and his talk a stimulating memory. From Edward's seventh to his fourteenth year, Cheke's influence was unparalleled partly because his attitude was more that of a scholar-companion than that of scholar-instructor, and partly because he gave his whole heart and mind to his pupil. Cheke was ambitious, watchful, sometimes critical, but never did he express himself harshly. Cheke taught as if he himself were discovering the subject for the first

[2] Hester W. Chapman, *The Last Tudor King,* Ulverscroft, Leicester, 1958.

time. In all this Cheke's spiritual influence and Bible knowledge were communicated most effectively.

The illuminating words of counsel that Cheke gave to *Lady Jane Grey* were probably given to Edward as well: "In hearing the word of God, whether it be by the voice of others or *by yourself reading*, you are ever to think that God speaketh to you . . .You are to remember that you speak to God . . .You walk in the eye and sight of God . . . when you speak to God, know that you speak to Him who understandeth the bottom of your heart." [3]

When his sister Mary was on a visit to the French ambassador, Edward in writing to Katherine Parr said, "Preserve, therefore, I pray you, my dear sister Mary, from all the wiles and enchantments of the evil one, and beseech her to attend no longer to foreign dances and merriments, which do not become a Christian princess . . ." This admonition illustrates the sobriety of mind which his tutor had instilled into the mind of the royal student.

Edward always enjoyed the visits of Elizabeth, for when she came she joined him in the classroom. The visits of Lady Jane Grey, were also a special delight. They were the same age and Edward thought that she was the smartest girl that he knew. Often the older girls would take the younger children to the park and play simple games with them.

[3] Mary Luke, *The Nine Days Queen,* William Morrow and Co., New York, 1986.

Edward's excellent and learned tutors gave full attention to their distinguished charge. But in the instruction and growth of this splendid young prince, the influence of Cranmer, the Archbishop of Canterbury must never be forgotten. The watchful care of that excellent man of God, and his great concerns for the progress of the Reformation, were continually exercised for the benefit of the heir to the throne, and for his solid advancement in true Christianity and sound Bible learning.

Archbishop Cranmer, Edward's godfather, kept up a close relationship with Edward as may be seen in their exchange of letters. Edward's letter to Cranmer is noteworthy, "Although I am but a child, yet I am not unmindful of the services and the kindnesses you daily perform and manifest towards me. I have not forgotten your kind letters delivered to me on St. Peter's eve. I was unwilling to answer them until now, not from neglect or forgetfulness, but that, as I daily meditated on them, and committed their contents faithfully to memory, at length having well considered them I might reply the more wisely. I do indeed embrace and venerate the truly paternal affection towards me which is expressed in them—may your life be prolonged for many years, and may you continue to be a respected father to me by your godly and wholesome counsels. For I consider that godliness is to be desired and embraced by me above all things, since St. Paul said, 'Godliness is profitable unto all things' " (1 Tim. 4:8). [4]

Cranmer's reply, also written in Latin, reveals the close spirtitual bond that existed between them, "My beloved son in Christ—I am as much concerned for your welfare as my own . . . . Your letters are pleasing to me. They show that you possess a disposition worthy of your rank, and a preceptor suitable for such a disposition. From your letters I perceive that you so cultivate learning that heavenly truths are not among the things you least care for, and whoso careth for those things shall not be overcome by any cares. Go on, therefore, in the way upon which you have entered, and adorn your native land, that the light of virtue, which I behold in you, may hereafter enlighten all your England." [5]

The manner in which the labors of these servants of God were blessed in the life of Prince Edward is superbly stated by *William Thomas,* himself a learned man, and who later became clerk of the Privy Council, which was the government of England during Edward's minority. In a work entitled "The Pilgrim," he says, "If you knew the eagerness of that young prince, your hearts would melt to hear him named, and you would abhor the malice of them that wish him ill. The most beautiful boy that liveth under the sun; the wittiest, the most amiable and the gentlest

[4] *Writings of Edward the Sixth,* The Religious Tract Society, London, 1831.

[5] Ibid.

creature of all the world. Such a capacity in learning the things taught him by his schoolmasters, that it is a wonder to hear. He hath such a grace of posture, and gesture in gravity, when he comes into your presence, that it should seem he were already a father, and yet he is not the age of ten year." [6]

Curio, the Italian reformer said "that by their united praycrs, counsels and industry, they had formed a king of the highest, even of divine hopes." [7]

The Bible was his constant study and delight and he memorized whole passages. Most mature Christian workers must have recognized that there was more than natural obedience and teachableness that prepared the youthful prince to receive and appropriate the teachings of his able and spirtually-minded instructors. There was at work in the heart and mind of this dear boy the influence of the Holy Spirit who always presides whenever the word of God is understood and believed. Without this, human teachers plant and water in vain, because it is God who "gives the increase" (1 Cor. 3:7).

We gather from the general progress in Edward's life that somewhere about this time Edward recognized his need and trusted Christ as Savior. He must have believed that the death of Jesus, the Son of God, on the cross was the completely sufficient payment for his sins. During Edward's reign, these

[6] Ibid.

[7] Ibid.

precious truths of Christ's meditorial work, so long obscured by the mists of wrong teaching, were being recovered and spread across Europe by the great reformers.

It might have been a Scripture like John 1:12 that clearly directed him to the Savior: "But as many as received Him, to them gave He the power to become the sons of God, even to them that believed on His name." In writing his thesis on the Primacy of the Pope, we see how clearly Edward understood the Gospel. He said, "We see therefore, that the Gospel revealed in the Holy Scriptures is the only gate to the kingdom of God," and again he writes, "And in the fourth chapter to the Romans, he saith, 'But to him that worketh not, but believeth on Him that justifieth the ungodly, his faith is counted for righteousness' (Rom. 4:5)." Edward knew these Scriptures and there is ample evidence in his life that he also knew the Lord personally as his Savior.

It is highly possible that in the course of his training Edward might have been exposed to the enlightening theological duel between *Sir Thomas More* and *William Tyndale.*

MORE: Christ said not, the Holy Ghost shall *write,* but shall *teach.* Whatsoever the church says, it is the word of God, though it be not in Scripture.

TYNDALE: It is not the custom of Scripture to say the Holy Ghost writeth but inspireth the writer . . . and it is manifest that . . . love compelled the apostles to leave nothing unwritten that should be necessarily required, and that, if it were left out, should hurt the soul . . . . *These are written,* says St. John, *that ye may believe and through belief have life.* (1 Jn. 2:1; Rom. 15:4; Matt. 22:29).

MORE: The apostles have taught by mouth many things they did not write, because they should not come into the hands of the heathen for mocking.

TYNDALE: I pray you what thing more to be mocked by the heathen could they teach than the resurrection; and that Christ was God and man, and died between two thieves? And yet all these things the apostles wrote. And again, purgatory, penance, and satisfaction for sin, and praying to saints, are marvellously agreeable unto the superstition of the heathen people, so that they needed not to abstain from writing of them for fear lest the heathen should have mocked them.

MORE: We must not examine the teaching of the church by Scripture, but understand Scripture by means of what the church says.

TYNDALE: What! Does the air give light to the sun, or the sun to the air? Is the church before the gospel, or the gospel before the church? Is not the father older than the son? *God begat us with his own will, with the word of truth,* says St. James (1:18). If he who begetteth is before him who is begotten, the *word* is before the *church,* or, to speak more correctly, before the *congregation.*

MORE: Why do you say *congregation* and not *church?*

TYNDALE: Because by that word *church,* you understand nothing but a multitude of shaven, shorn and oiled, which we now call the spiritualty or clergy; while the word of right is common unto all the congregation of them that believe in Christ.

MORE: The church is the pope and his sect or followers.

TYNDALE: The pope teacheth us to trust in holy works for salvation, as penance, saint's merits, and friars' coats. Now, he that hath no faith to be saved through Christ, is not of Christ's church.

MORE: The Romish church from which the Lutherans came out, was before them, and therefore is the right one.

TYNDALE: In like manner you may say, the church of the Pharisees, whence Christ and His apostles came out, was before them, and was therefore the right church, and consequently Christ and his disciples are heretics.

MORE: No: the apostles came out from the church of the Pharisees because they found not Christ there; but your priests in Germany and elsewhere, have come out of our church, because they wanted wives.

TYNDALE: Wrong . . . these priests were at first

took wives; but yours were first attached to the holy doctrine of the pope, and then they took harlots.

MORE: Luther's books be open, if ye will not believe us.

TYNDALE: Nay, ye have shut them up, and have even burnt them . . . .

MORE: I marvel that you deny purgatory, Sir William, except it be a plain point with you to go straight to hell.

TYNDALE: I know no other purging but faith in the cross of Christ; while you, for a groat or a sixpence, buy some secret pills [indulgences] which you take to purge yourselves of your sins.

MORE: Faith, then, is your purgatory, you say; there is no need, therefore, of works—a most immoral doctrine!

TYNDALE: It is faith alone that saves us, but not a bare faith. When a horse beareth a saddle and a man thereon, we may well say that the horse only and alone beareth the saddle, but we do not mean the saddle empty, and no man thereon.[8]

In this manner did the catholic and the evangelical carry on the discussion. According to Tyndale, what constitutes the true church is the work of the Holy Ghost within; according to More, the constitution of the papacy without. The spiritual character

---

[8] J. H. Merle D'Aubigne, *The Reformation in England,* Vol. 1, Banner of Truth Trust, London, 1962, pp. 394-396.

of the gospel is thus put in opposition to the formalist character of the Roman church. The Reformation restored to our belief the solid foundation of the Word of God; for the sand it substituted the rock. [9]

This would have been a heavy dose of doctrine, but Edward, though young in years, was well able to grapple with it.

Edward's education was not spiritual and literary alone. In 1551 Cheke designed for him an astronomical quadrant. In his father's residences Edward was surrounded by maps and globes which he studied with enthusiasm. [10]

We came across an incident which reveals his devotion to the principles in which he was being trained. He was engaged with his companions in some amusements and wished to take down from a shelf something above his reach. One of his friends offered him a large Bible to stand upon. Perceiving it was a Bible, Edward verily exploded with indignation. He sharply reproved his friend and added that it was improper that he should trample under his feet that which ought to be treasured in the mind and heart.

During this period of his life the prince resided chiefly in Hertfordshire. Remarkable progress was made in his education. He wrote letters in Latin and in French as early as his ninth year. There are also

[9] Ibid.

[10] Jennifer Loach, *Edward VI*, Yale University Press, New Haven, 1999.

31

several Latin orations and themes by the prince which are preserved in the British Museum.

The prince seems to have enjoyed life at the royal court. Like his father, Edward liked music and could play the flute and perhaps other instruments as well. He was probably taught by one of his father's most favored musicians, the Netherlandish lutenist, *Philip van der Wilder,* who was a member of Edward's privy chamber.

About this time, a learned Italian, named *Cardano,* visited England on his return from Scotland to the continent. He had an interview with the king, and has left a beautiful testimony respecting England's youthful monarch: "All the graces are combined in him. He possesses the knowledge of many languages while yet a child. In addition to English, his native tongue, he is well acquainted both with Latin and French, nor is he ignorant of the Greek, Latin, Italian and Spanish, and perhaps others. He was also acquainted with the principles of natural philosophy, and with of music; he played the lute well. A beautiful specimen of mortality; his seriousness manifested royal majesty; his disposition was suitable to his exalted rank. In sum, that young lad was so educated, possessed such abilities, and caused such expectations, that he appeared a miracle. This is not said as mere rhetorical expressions, nor does it exceed the truth, but in fact falls short of it." [11]

[11] *Writings of Edward the Sixth*, 1831.

In a letter from *John Hooper,* bishop of Glouchester to Bullinger, son-in-law of the Swiss Protestant leader, *Zwingli,* he wrote, "Believe me, my much esteemed friend, you have never seen in the world for these thousand years so much erudition united with piety and sweetness of disposition. Should he live and grow up with these virtues, he will be a terror to all the sovereigns of the earth. He receives with his own hand a copy of every sermon that he hears, and most diligently requires an account of them after dinner from those who study with him. Many of the boys and youths who are his companions in study are well and faithfully instructed in the fear of God and in good learning." [12]

[12] C. R. N. Routh, *They Saw it Happen,* Basil Blackwell, Oxford, 1956.

≈ *4* ≈

The Accession and Coronation of King Edward VI

Immediately after the death of Henry VIII, *Edward Seymour* (Lord Hertford) and *Sir Anthony Browne* left for Ashridge where young Edward was residing. Instead of telling him at once of his father's death, Seymour took *Edward* to Enfield, where his sister *Elizabeth* lived. Kneeling before the prince Seymour told him of his father's death and that he was now king of England. Edward and Elizabeth clung to each other and burst into a passion of tears. "Never," says Edward's first biographer, "was sorrow more sweetly set forth, their faces seeming to beautify their sorrow." They all cried together for a long time.

They spent the rest of the day and night at Enfield and next morning they set out for the Tower of London where he would remain until the coronation three weeks later. During the time preceding his coronation Edward kept himself busy by writing letters. Cheke joined him at the Tower and helped Edward in phrasing his notes, especially those that were being sent to the Emperor of the Holy Roman Empire and other individuals in positions of power.

As the preparations were being made for the coronation procession, the piety of the youthful monarch was shown in an incident that is worth remembering. *John Bale* relates, upon the authority of credible witnesses, that when three swords were brought to be carried in the procession, as emblematic of his three kingdoms, the king said "there was one yet wanting."

The nobles inquired what it was and he answered, "The Bible," and then added, "That book is the sword of the Spirit, and to be preferred before these swords. That ought in all right to govern us, who use them for the people's safety by God's appointment. Without that sword we are nothing, we can do nothing, we have not power. From the Bible we are what we are this day. From it we receive whatsoever it is that we at present do assume. He that rules without it, is not to be called God's minister or king. Under the Bible, the word of God, we ought to live, to fight, to govern the people and to perform all our affairs. From it alone we obtain all power, virtue, grace, salvation and whatsoever we have of divine strength."[1]

[1] *Writings of Edward the Sixth*, The Religious Tract Society, London, 1831.

In the long and varied history of England, it may be said without fear of contradiction that no other monarch approached his or her coronation with such spiritual perception and with such solid conviction as to the authority and power of the word of God; more amazing still is the fact that this king was only nine years of age at the time of his coronation.

When the devout young king had thus expressed himself, he commanded that the Bible be brought and carried it before him with the greatest reverence.

No doubt, many who heard such words rejoiced and exclaimed fervently, "Praise the Lord."

The day before Edward's coronation at Westminster Abbey there was the procession from the Tower to the Palace of Westminster. Only the higher clergy and nobility were in the procession, and now for the first time Edward made his public and official entry among the people as their ruler. He rode on horseback and was dressed in a gown of cloth of silver embroidered in gold with a belt set with rubies, diamonds and pearls; his white velvet cap was set with diamonds and pearls. His uncle Edward Seymour, now the duke of Somerset, rode on his left. As the king entered Mark Lane—the city frontier—a peal of cannon sounded from the arsenal in the tower.

The first stop was at Frenchurch Street, where a

choir standing on an ornamental scaffold gave a recital of sacred music. Two children stepped forward and addressed Edward in a bit of rhyme:

> Hail, noble Edward, our King and sovereign,
> Hail, the chief comfort of your commonalty
> Hail, redolent rose, whose sweetness to retain
> Ye unto us all such great commodity. [2]

Some author observed that what these lines lacked in syntax and precision they made up in loving fervour.

Thereafter, love and loyalty gushed out from all directions and many joined in the refrain, "God save the king." After some three hours, the procession stopped at the Cross in Cheapside, where the Mayor stepped forward, kneeling, presented Edward with a large purse containing a thousand crowns. Other spectacles followed until after some four hours they arrived at the Palace of Westminster. During the latter half of the procession, the ballad that was sung throughout his realm "echoed the refrain that carried with it the love and hope of the humble and the obscure":

> "Sing up, heart, sing up, heart and sing no more down,
> For joy of King Edward, that weareth the crown!

> Your song in time past hath been down-a-down,
> And long it hath lasted in town and town.

> To very much metre Down hath been added,
> But Up is now sweeter, to make our hearts gladded.

[2] Mary M. Luke, *A Crown For Elizabeth*, Coward-McMann, Inc., N. Y., 1970.

Ye children of England, for joy of the same,
Take bow and shaft in hand, learn shootage to frame,

That you another day may so do your parts,
As to serve your King as well with hands as with hearts.

Ye children that are towards, wing up and down,
And never play the cowards to him that weareth the crown,

But always do your cure his pleasure to fulfill,
Then shall you keep right sure the honour of England still.

Sing up, heart, sing up, heart, and sing no more down,
For joy of King Edward, that weareth the crown!" [3]

At Westminster Palace Edward slept in the great bedchamber where his father had died holding Cranmer's hand.

The next day Edward, robed in his surcoat, train and gown of crimson velvet embroidered in gold and furred with miniver, and his attendants proceeded by foot to Westminster Abbey. Edward moved alone and sat on St. Edward's Chair. Cranmer, who had been awaiting him at the altar rails, turned to the nobles and clergy and proclaimed: "Sirs, here present is Edward, rightful and undoubted inheritor by the laws of God and man to the crown and royal dignity of this realm . . . Will you serve at this time and give your wills and consents to the same consecration, enunction and coronation?"

The reply came formally and fervently, "Yea! Yea! Yea! God save King Edward!" Edward then proceeded

[3] W. K. Jordan, *Edward VI: The Young King*, Harvard University Press, Cambridge, MA., 1968.

to the high altar where Cranmer was kneeling. After a short pause Edward lay prostrate while Archbishop Cranmer repeated the litany. Edward then approached the altar for the anointing of arms, breast, back, forehead and hands.

Edward once more took his seat in St. Edward's Chair. He was then crowned with three crowns— that of St. Edward, with the Crown Imperial, which is too sacred to be altered and which was held over his head, and finally with a smaller reproduction of the Crown Imperial that had been made to fit his head. Between each crowning the trumpets sounded.

Then Cranmer turned to the young monarch, speaking to him alone, but loud enough for every one in the Abbey to hear. The great coronation address is included here in full because this was the first monarch of England in recent centuries to be crowned without the authority of the pope in Rome:

"Most venerable and royal sovereign; the promises your highness hath made here, at your coronation, to forsake the devil and all his works, are not to be taken in the bishop of Rome's sense; when you commit anything distasteful to that see, to hit your majesty in the teeth, as pope Paul the third, late bishop of Rome, sent to your royal father, saying, 'Didst thou not promise, at our permission of thy coronation, to forsake the devil and all his works, and dost thou run to heresy? For the breach of this thy promise, knowest thou not, that it is in our power to dispose of thy sword and sceptre to whom we please?'

"We, your majesty's clergy, do humbly conceive, that this promise reacheth not at Your Highness's sword, spiritual or temporal, or in the least at Your Highness swaying sceptre of this your dominion, as you and your predecessors have had them from God. Neither could your ancestors lawfully resign up their crowns to the bishop of Rome or his legates, according to their ancient oaths then taken upon that ceremony.

"The bishops of Canterbury, for the most part, have crowned your predecessors, and anointed them kings of this land; yet it was not in their power to receive or reject them; neither did it give them authority to prescribe them conditions to take or leave their crowns, although the bishops of Rome would encroach upon your predecessors, by their act and oil, that in the end they might possess those bishops with an interest to dispose of their crowns at their pleasure. But the wiser sort will look to their claws and clip them.

"The solemn rites of coronation have their ends and utility; yet neither direct force or necessity: they are good admonitions to put kings in mind of their duty to God, but no increasement of their dignity; for they are God's anointed; not in respect of the oil which the bishop useth, but in consideration of their power, which is ordained; of the sword, which is authorized; of their persons, which are elected of God, and endued with the gifts of His Spirit, for the better ruling and guiding of His people.

"The oil, if added, is but a ceremony: if it be wanting, that king is yet a perfect monarch notwithstanding, and God's anointed, as well as if he was not anointed. Now for the person or bishop that doth anoint a king, it is proper to be done by the chiefest. But if they cannot, or will not, any bishop may perform this ceremony.

"To condition with monarchs upon these ceremonies, the bishop of Rome (or other bishops owning his supremacy) hath no authority; but he may faithfully declare what God requires at the hands of kings and rulers, that is, religion and virtue. Therefore, not from the bishop of Rome, but as a messenger from my Savior Jesus Christ, I shall most humbly admonish your Royal Majesty, what things your highness is to perform.

"Your Majesty is God's vicegerent [administrative deputy], and Christ's vicar within your own dominions, and to see, with your predecessor Josiah, God truly worshipped, and idolatry destroyed; the tyranny of the bishops of Rome banished from your subjects, and images removed. These acts are signs of a second Josiah, who reformed the people of God in his days. [Actually Edward was already Josiah who desired 'God truly worshipped and idolatry destroyed.'] You are to reward virtue, to revenge sin, to justify the innocent, to relieve the poor, to procure peace, to repress violence, and to execute justice throughout your realms.

"For precedents on those kings who performed not these things, the old law shows how the Lord revenged His quarrel; and on those kings who fulfilled these things, He poured forth His blessings in abundance. For example, it is written of Josiah, in the book of the Kings, thus: 'Like unto him there was no king, that turned to the Lord with all his heart, according to all the law of Moses; neither after him arose there any like him' (2 Kings 23:25). This was to that prince a perpetual fame of dignity, to remain to the end of days.

"Being bound by my function to lay these things before your royal highness; the one, as a reward if you fulfil; the other, as a judgment from God if you neglect them; yet I openly declare, before the living God, and before these nobles of the land, that I have no commission to denounce your majesty deprived, if your highness miss in part, or in whole, of these performances; much less to draw up indentures between God and your majesty; or to say you forfeit your crown, with a clause for the bishop of Rome, as have been done by your majesty's predecessors, King John and his son Henry of this land.

"The Almighty God of His mercy let the light of His countenance shine upon your majesty, grant you a prosperous and happy reign, defend you, and save you; and let your subjects say, 'Amen. GOD SAVE THE KING.' "[4]

Following Cranmer's address a coronation banquet was held at Westminster Hall which lasted some four hours. Edward then left the table and went down the hall to receive the Ministers of State and the foreign ambassadors. The young king was regal in the grace, patience and interest in all those with whom he conversed, either in Latin or French, or in English. One of the envoys remarked, "It should seem he were already a father, yet passes not the age of ten years."

[4] *Writings of Edward the Sixth,* 1831.

43

≈ 5 ≈

The Settlement of Power During the King's Minority

Prior to his death on January 28th, King Henry VIII appointed twenty-eight men to form the Privy Council which would rule the realm until Edward reached the age of eighteen. Those who were appointed to this Council were as follows:

Edward Seymour, Earl of Hertford, then Duke of Somerset
William Paulet, Lord St. John of Basing, Great Master of the Household
Thomas Cranmer, Archbishop of Canterbury
Sir John Russell, Keeper of the Privy Seal
William Parr, Earl of Essex
John Dudley, Viscount Lisle, Lord Admiral, later Earl of Warwick, then
   Duke of Northumberland
Henry Fitzalan, 12th Earl of Arundel, Lord Chamberlain of the Household
Sir Thomas Seymour, later Lord Admiral
Cuthbert Tunstall, Bishop of Durham
Thomas Wriothesley, Chancellor, shortly replaced by
   Sir Richard Rich
Sir John Gage, Comptroller of the Household
Sir Anthony Browne (d. 1548), Master of the Horse
Sir Anthony Wingfield, Vice-Chamberlain
Sir William Paget, Principal Secretary

Sir William Petre, Principal Secretary
Sir Ralph Sadler, Master of the Wardrobe
Sir John Baker, Speaker of the House of Commons
Dr. Nicholas Wotton, Dean of Canterbury and of York
Sir Anthony Denny (d. 1549), Gentleman of the Privy Chamber
Sir William Herbert, Gentleman of the Privy Chamber
Sir Edward North, Chancellor of the Court of Augmentations
Sir Edward Montague, Chief Justice of Common Pleas
Sir Edward Wotton, Treasurer of Calais
Sir Edmond Peckham, Cofferer of the Household
Sir Thomas Bromley, Justice of Common Pleas
Sir Richard Southwell

The Privy Council met on January 31st and again on February 1st. They solemnly called upon God for aid. Although King Henry's will did not authorize the appointment of one man as Protector, neither did it seem to prohibit such action. Paget, who had been very close to Henry VIII in the months preceding his death, urged the wisdom and necessity for giving one special man primacy among the group in order to expedite affairs of state.

Since Henry intended that the Privy Council as a whole should reign during Edward's minority, it was Paget "who supplied the momentum, the skill, and the audacity required to bridge the gulf between the two reigns and to deposit an immense aggregate of power in Somerset's hands . . . only he and Somerset knew that undergirding their relation was the private agreement that Paget would in effect be the first minister to the Lord Protector." [1]

[1] W. K. Jordan, *Edward VI: The Young King,* Harvard University Press, Cambridge, MA., 1968.

45

It was declared that Edward Seymour (Edward's maternal uncle) in view of the close affinity in blood with the king and his long experience in the conduct of the affairs of the realm, should be that "special man," being in name and title "Protector of all the realms and dominions" of the king and governor of the king's person. It was sad and unfortunate that this agreement was not maintained by Seymour.

This technically violated the will of Henry VIII as expressed in his letter, but it made the intention of the king workable. Edward in his *Chronicle 4* deals briefly but accurately with what transpired: "The next day, being the 31st of January, he (the king) was brought to the Tower of London, where he tarried the space of three weeks; and in the mean season the Council sat every day for the performance of the will . . . At length they thought best to choose the duke of Somerset (Edward Seymour) to be Protector of the realm and Governor of the king's person . . . during the minority, to which all the gentlemen and lords did agree, because he was the king's uncle on his mother's side."

On February 1st, 1547, the Council announced to Edward their action in appointing the duke of Somerset as Protector. At that moment Edward gave his assent to the appointment.

To make the change in government, legal care was taken to secure from the king a signed commission which with all the Council's names appended was passed under the Great Seal as a warrant for sovereign power until such time as the king should have reached the age of eighteen.

The appointment of Somerset as Protector was very crucial both for the sake of the young king and for the advancement of the Reformation. Somerset's spiritual stature is clearly noticeable in his prayer which he seemed to have kept before him during his time of leadership:

"O my Lord and my God, I am the price of Thy son's death, Jesus Christ; for His sake Thou wilt keep me. I am recorded in the Book of Life, I am written with the very blood of Jesus; Thy inestimable love will not cancel then my name.

"Thou, Lord by Thy providence hast called me to rule; make me able therefore to follow Thy calling. Thou, Lord, by Thine order hast committed an anointed king to my governance; direct me therefore with Thy hand, that I err not from Thy good pleasure. Finish in me Thy beginning, and begin in me that which Thou wilt finish.

"By Thee do kings reign, and from Thee all power is derived. Govern me, Lord, as I shall govern; rule me, as I shall rule . . . I am by appointment Thy minister for Thy king, a shepherd for Thy people, a sword-bearer for Thy justice. I am ready, Lord, to do what Thou dost command; command what Thou wilt. Teach me what to ask, and then give me that I ask.

"I ask for victory, but to show Thy power upon the wicked. I ask prosperity, but for to rule in peace Thy congregation. I ask wisdom, but by my council to set forth Thy cause. And, as I ask for myself, so, Lord, pour Thy knowledge upon all them who shall counsel me . . . Thus I conclude, Lord, by the name of Thy son Jesus Christ." [2]

Somerset's chief occupation at the outset was to conciliate bisops, particularly Gardiner in order to make some progress with the Reformation. His regime faced three hostile constituencies: the Emperor, Charles V, the majority of the lay people in the nation and those bishops who were not part of the Reformation inner circle.

In the first month of Edward's reign, the three chief Council members who dominated things were *Cranmer, Somerset* and the *earl of Warwick.* Paget worked closely with them.

Within a few weeks *Wriothesley* was ousted and the Great Seal was handed over to Somerset.

Edward continued his training under Cheke who had him beginning Plutarch's *Apophthegms, Morals* and *Lives.* Then came geometry and Italian, geography and Latin. His English reading was still mainly that of the Bible. *Roger Ascham*, came several times a week for the writing lessons that the king

[2] *Writings of Edward the Sixth*, The Religious Tract Society, London, 1831.

48

still found rather irksome. The matter of swearing came up in which both Edward and a friend were involved. Since one dare not lay hands on the Lord's anointed, Edward stood by while his friend was whipped. Cheke told the king that the fault was really his, and that if he were heard swearing again, his status would be ignored, and he himself would receive the beating.

The Fall of Thomas Seymour

While Somerset was busy with the great matters of the realm, he seemed to have very little time for the young king. This is where *Thomas Seymour,* (the younger brother of Edward Seymour, the duke of Somerset) who became Lord Admiral, moved in, always on the lookout for what might profit him in the end. Seymour sounded out the king on how he would feel if he, the Admiral, married the Queen-Dowager, Katherine Parr, who was King Henry's last wife. Edward wrote to Katherine on his uncle's behalf and in March the couple exchanged rings.

Somerset worked long days on the treaty with the Scots in trying to enforce the marriage of *Mary Stuart* (Queen of Scots and Edward's cousin) with Edward. While Somerset was preparing for a war with Scotland by land and by sea, the other members of the Admiralty Board told him that Thomas Seymour's behavior was approaching treason. Instead of dismissing him, Somerset was lenient and simply reprimanded him. The Admiral chafed and stamped about for a while and set out a scheme whereby he could win the favor of the young king.

He saw that his brother, Somerset, had begun an economy campaign and allowed the king little or no pocket money. This is where the Admiral stepped in and supplied the king with any sum, large or small, that the king needed or wanted. He reminded the king, "If His Highness lacks money, send to me for it and nobody else."

The Protector (Somerset) was far too busy to attend Edward's getting up and going to bed. His interviews with his nephew, the king, took place after Council meetings and at state banquets. This gave Thomas Seymour more opportunity to poison Edward's mind against Somerset. In fact Edward began to wonder if he were king in name only, and he said at one point, "My uncle, Somerset dealeth very hardly with me, and keepeth me so straight that I cannot have money at my will. But my Lord Admiral both sends me money, and gives me money." [3]

Somerset went to Scotland again, but without success, for in July 1548 the little Queen of Scots was smuggled out of the kingdom into France. All the while Thomas Seymour pressed Edward for favors until the king, exasperated, said, "Let me alone." Thomas Seymour kept showing these favors to

[3] Hester W. Chapman, *The Last Tudor King*, Ulverscroft, Leicester, 1958.

Edward and finally he asked Edward to sign a request to the Council that the Protectorate be transferred from Somerset to himself (Thomas Seymour), Edward refused and Cheke cautioned Edward not to become involved in any of the requests coming from the Admiral.

Thomas Seymour was becoming desperate and went from one Council member to another with the suggestion that he become the Protector instead of his brother. When his wife Katherine died, he began making advances to Elizabeth, sister of Edward. The Admiral fascinated her, but he was not worth the risk of imprisonment and disgrace that would have been the result of her marrying him without permission of the Privy Council.

Since it was becoming more difficult to see Edward alone, the Admiral, on the night of January 16th, 1549, armed with a pistol, took two of his servants, and let himself into the Privy Garden and so reached the king's bedchamber without passing through the ante-chambers and passages. When everyone was asleep the king had made his way out of bed and bolted the inner door on his own side, having put his little dog beyond the outer side. As soon as the Admiral began fumbling with the lock, the dog sprang up barking furiously. Maddened and desperate, Seymour shot the dog. This brought in an army of attendants. There stood the Admiral, with the smoking pistol in his hand. To the torrents of questions, he could only mumble, "I wished to know whether His Majesty was safely guarded." Within a few minutes he was under arrest.

It was for such a moment as this that the earl of Warwick had been waiting, for he himself aspired, in time, to supplant Somerset as Protector. Somerset recommended an open trial but at once that was blocked by Warwick and others. At first the Admiral indulged in denials with defiance and contempt. He kept thinking that His Majesty would stand for him.

Several weeks passed following the signing of the warrant for the execution of the Admiral. The Council members came to Edward's Presence-Chamber and knelt to hear Edward's reply. It came quickly and decidedly: "I have well perceived your proceedings therein, and give you my hearty thanks for your pains and travail, and great care you have for my surety. I will and command you that you proceed as you request without further molestation of myself, or of the Lord Protector, I pray you my Lords, do so." [4]

A few hours later he signed the warrant and the Admiral was taken to the scaffold where he was executed. The popular feeling rose in the Admiral's favor—exactly as Warwick had calculated. Somerset was spoken of by the public as a "blood-sucker and a ravenous wolf." However, a few days after Thomas Seymour's execution, bishop Latimer,

[4] Ibid.

preaching before the king and Protector, concluded his sermon with a diatribe against the Admiral, whom he described as "a man furthest from the fear of God than any man in England. He was a covetous man; he was a seditious man, a contemner of common prayer—I would there were no more in England. Well! He is gone! *I would he had left none behind him."* [5]

[5] Ibid.

6

King Edward
and His Overseers

Somerset tried to rush through his reforms in line with the Protestant faith, and he often became impatient with the Council members in his efforts. Edward was left to take in the heady mixture of religious attacks for political ends that Somerset dispensed, and this brought confusion to the earnest young king, and tended to estrange him from the Protector, his uncle. Many of the changes Somerset initiated were good, but the people, steeped in Romanism and ignorance, did not understand nor appreciate them.

There was always opposition to Somerset's proposals in the Council. *Hugh Latimer*, a bishop and the most outspoken and popular among the preachers, tried often to curb the opposition in his sermons at Westminster. Inveighing against corruption in high places, of which Thomas Seymour was an example, he declared that it was partly the lust for power, to which all succumbed, adding, "There be some wicked people that will say, 'Tush, this gear will not tarry; it is but my Lord Protector's and my Lord of Canterbury's doing; the king is but a child, and he knoweth not of it . . .' Jesu, mercy! What people are they that say, 'The king is but a child?' Have we not a noble king? So godly— brought up with so noble councillors, so excellent and well learned schoolmasters? I will tell you this, and I will speak it even as I think—His Majesty hath more godly wit and knowledge at this age, than twenty of his progenitors—that I could name—had, at any time of their life." [1]

Then, addressing Edward directly, he went on to warn him against pride and begged him to drive away "flatterers and claw-backs." "Hear men's suits yourself," he urged, "I require you in God's behalf; and put it not to the hearing of these velvet coats, these upskips. I beseech Your Grace that ye will look to these matters—hear them yourself." [2]

Cheke also had a concern for the king in his rapid learning. In a letter to Somerset, he said, "Wherefore, as his majesty has always learned, so I trust he laboureth daily to avoid the ground of all error, that self-pleasing which the Greeks call *Philautia*, and

[1] Hester W. Chapman, *The Last Tudor King,* Ulverscroft, Leicester, 1958.

[2] Ibid.

which occurs when a man delighteth in his own reason and despiseth other men's counsel, and thinketh no man's foresight to be so good as his, nor any man's judgment compared to his own."[3]

Stephen Gardiner, bishop of Winchester, had worried the Protestants of the Council; they asked the bishop to preach a sermon. This he did, and as might have been expected, he emphasized the Roman Catholic doctrine of "transubstantiation," wherein Christ's body and blood are actually present in the Eucharist. He accused the extreme Protestants of blasphemy in their denial of the Real Presence, and then added, "I mislike subjects that rule like kings, to the diminishing of the king's authority, and their own estate—I have but one king (as he pointed to Edward), and he only to be obeyed!"[4] And for his adamant Romanism the ruling Council sent Gardiner to the Tower as prisoner on February 15, 1547.

The heresy laws were abolished in 1547, including the *Act of Six Articles* enacted under Henry VIII. Now further steps in the Reformation could be taken. Celibacy for the clergy began to be frowned upon and was eliminated finally by Parliament in 1549.

In April 1547, the Emperor, Charles V, shattered Protestant power in Germany in a decisive victory

[3] *Writings of Edward the Sixth,* The Religious Tract Society, London, 1831.

[4] Hester W. Chapman, *The Last Tudor King,* 1958.

over the *Schmalkaldic League* at Muhlberg. This brought dismay in London. However the regime of Edward picked up the threads of its program, and the "Homilies" were finally published in 1548. Here it was stated emphatically that justification was *by faith alone.*

In furtherance of Henry VIII's own policy as well as Somerset's zeal for bringing Protestantism to Scotland, Somerset wished to unite England, Scotland, Wales and Ireland and give Edward the title of Emperor of Great Britain.

To understand the Scots we need to recall that in 1542, Henry VIII defeated Scotland in the great battle of Solway Moss where *James V*, king of Scotland (see family tree) was killed. Having destroyed the Scottish military power, Henry began immediately to apply heavy pressure on the Scots to secure a binding treaty of marriage alliance between his son, Edward, then six years of age, and *Mary Stuart*, infant daughter of James V. His ultimate aim was to secure the union of Scotland and England. However, the Queen Mother, widow of James V, favored a French alliance for her daughter for she was Marie or *Mary Guise* of Lorraine, of a powerful family of the French ruling class. A Roman Catholic, she disdained Protestantism which she called the "New Religion."

In 1551, the Queen Dowager and Regent of Scotland had requested a passage of safe conduct through England after her ship was stormbound on its southern coast. Although Edward was disappointed because the Queen Dowager's daughter, Mary Stuart, known as the Queen of Scots, would not be his wife, he and the Council showed her great hospitality. Edward directed that the mother of little Mary Stuart not only be given safe passage, but with "special honors." She was welcomed with a great display of kindness and hospitality. At the dinner Edward lamented that Mary Stuart would wed the French Dauphin. He spoke of the treaty that the Queen Dowager had made with his father and how he thought the treaty should be renewed and that he would treat her daughter with great kindness. The Queen Dowager reminded Edward of the bloody excursions that the Protector had made into Scotland and that such behavior nullified the contract, saying with some measure of amusement, "Such a fashion of dealing is not the nearest way to conquer a lady."[5]

During the war between Scotland and France, *John Knox*, the great reformer of Scotland, was taken prisoner and shipped off to France and there he was made a galley-slave where he was subjected to jibes and insults, hard treatment and terrible exposure. On one occasion, he was asked by his abusive companions to kiss a wooden figure of the Virgin Mary. Treating the request with deserved

[5] Mary Luke, *The Nine Days Queen,* William Morrow and Co., New York, 1986.

58

contempt, Knox cast the wooden idol overboard exclaiming, as he did so,—"Let our Lady save herself, she is light enough—let her learn to swim."

In the second year of his reign, King Edward had Knox and many others released from the French bondage and had them brought to England. Knox preached at the court with great faithfulness. His preaching was especially appreciated by the king.

England's beneficial interests were to be found in a marriage between Edward VI and Mary, Queen of Scots, rather than in such alliances with France, which Northumberland proposed. Northumberland made peace with Scotland, but it must be observed that Somerset's efforts were not in vain because they fostered elements which eventually produced success in uniting England and Scotland. During the English occupation, the seeds of the Reformation in Scotland were sown, and it forced the Roman Catholics of Scotland into the arms of France. In turn the Roman Catholic cause became linked with that of French domination. National sentiment in Scotland was evoked against the French and the Protestant party became the national party of Scotland, and Knox, the protege of Somerset and King Edward, the national hero. When Elizabeth came to the throne of England, she supported the Protestant party in Scotland. This enabled the Scots to expel the French, and the Protestant party became the dominant religious party of Scotland. Thus the difference of religion between England and Scotland was removed and paved the way for the union of the two realms.

All the problems which Somerset encountered tended to estrange him from the king. Struggling with an enfeebled army and navy, and an agricultural revolution, Somerset suffered attacks of bad temper. At Council meetings he stormed and threatened. Then fatally he began his great campaign against superstition and idolatry which the simple and untaught people did not understand. They were bewildered and confused. Somerset made the mistake of counting on his popularity to sweep the illiterate and poverty-stricken towards his intellectual concepts. Impoverished by the long Roman Catholic domination, the people did not have preachers like Latimer and Ridley. All they had were uninstructed priests trying to make sense out of Cranmer's *Book of Homilies*.

Hugh Latimer was the great attraction of the day. He was a philosopher, storyteller and Bible preacher. It is little wonder that Edward commanded him to speak again and again at Whitehall, where he appeared as a great actor in a pulpit set up in the Privy Garden, so that a thousand or more could listen. Old people, children and women sat on the grass just below him. Edward and Somerset sat at a window in the gallery facing the pulpit with Cheke standing behind them. Latimer kept his audience spellbound until he stopped to say "And now I would ask you a strange question—who is the most powerful prelate in all England; he surpasses all the rest in his diligence. I can tell you, for I know who it is; I know him well. But now I think I see you listening and hearkening that I should name him. And will you know who it is? I will tell you—it is the Devil. He is the most diligent preacher of all others; he is never out of his diocese . . . Call for him when you will, he is always available."[6]

Latimer boldly placed the law with its curses before his hearers, and then conjured them to flee to the Savior of the world. The same zeal which he had employed in saying mass, he now employed in preaching the true sacrifice of Christ. He said one day: "If one man had committed all the sins since Adam, you may be sure he should be punished with the same horror of death, in such a sort as all men in the world should have suffered . . . Such was the pain Christ endured . . . If our Savior had committed all the sins of the world; all that I for my part have done, all that you for your part have done, and that any man else hath done; if He had done all this himself, His agony that He suffered should have been no greater nor more grievous than it was . . . Believe in Jesus Christ, and you shall overcome death . . . But alas!" said he at another time, "the devil, by the help of that Italian bishop yonder, his chaplain, has labored by all means that he might frustrate the death

[6] Hester W. Chapman, *The Last Tudor King*, 1958.

of Christ and the merits of his passion." [7]

The Reformation was not the substitution of the catholicism of the first ages for the popery of the middle ages: it was a revival of the preaching of St. Paul, and thus it was that on hearing Latimer every-one exclaimed with rapture: "Of a *Saul*, God has made him a very *Paul*." [8]

Latimer had many adversaries. In the front rank were the priests, who spared no endeavors to retain souls in bondage. "Beware," said Latimer to the new converts, "lest robbers overtake you, and plunge you into the pope's prison of purgatory." [9]

[7] J. H. Merle d'Aubigne, *The Reformation in England,* Vol. 1, Banner of Truth Trust, London, 1853.

[8] Ibid.

[9] Ibid.

⋙7⋘

King Edward VI
Demonstrates Maturity

As we read the story of Edward VI, we are impressed with the fact that he never knew any adolescence. He was a "planting of the Lord" and grew in grace like a tree beside the rivers of water. His knowledge of the Scriptures and his delight in them was full of light and he passed from childhood to manhood—"a tree of righteousness," bearing fruit sixtyfold and a hundredfold.

From Edward's seventh to his fourteenth year, Cheke's influence was paramount, partly because his outlook was rather that of the scholar-companion than that of the courtier, and partly because he gave his whole heart and mind to his pupil for whom he was ambitious, watchful, sometimes critical but always gracious and kind. Cheke was in a unique position to counsel the young king in the affairs of state and in all the varied situations that came up in the king's dealings with the Council, with the foreign dignitaries and with all the people around him.

Cheke was seriously ill in 1552, and when his recovery was despaired of, Cheke wrote to Edward of his most important concerns: "Because I am departing," he said, "my sovereign lord, unto the King of all kings, Almighty God, and must by His appointment leave you, whom of long time I have done my best to bring up in virtue and good learning; and you are now coming to a government of yourself, in which state I pray God you may always be served with them that will faithfully, truly and plainly give you counsel, I have thought it my duty, for a memory of my last will and for a token of my well-wishing unto you, which now remains with me as it has heretofore done—to require you, yea, and in God's behalf, to charge you, that forasmuch as years both have and will diminish in you the fear of man, to have yet before your eyes continually the fear of God.

"By the which if you do not direct, order and temper all your doings and sayings, be you well assured neither to have good success in the great charge that He hath committed to you, neither in the end to enjoy that joyful place which is promised to them that fear Him. For if God do extremely punish men of low estate and of low degree, for wanting of that necessary jewel, which in the Scripture hath so many promises, how severely will he punish kings and princes failing therein, in whom the lack thereof must needs be perilous both to themselves and to the commonwealth." After other cautions and serious admonitions, Cheke further urges, "For your divinity, I would wish you would diligently continue the reading of the New Testament, with Sapientia, Ecclesiasticus and the Proverbs." [1]

The king deeply appreciated the words from Cheke and was most anxious for Cheke's recovery from the sweating sickness. Edward asked God for Cheke's healing in earnest prayer, and he must have really laid hold of the Scripture recorded in 1 John 5:15, "And if we know that He hear us, whatsoever we ask, we know that we have the petitions that we desired of Him." When told by the physicians that they despaired of his tutor's recovery, the king replied humbly but firmly, "No, Cheke will not die at this time. I begged God for his life this morning in my prayer, and obtained it." [2] This is one of the most remarkable instances of answered prayer that has ever come to my attention. It almost takes us back to the New Testament times when our Lord would make such declarations. The recovery of Cheke was regarded by the godly reformers as a national mercy. They knew not the darker hour which was approaching, both with respect to the tutor and his royal pupil.

[1] *Writings of Edward the Sixth*, The Religious Tract Society, London, 1831.

[2] Ibid.

65

Edward again showed his spirit of understanding and compassion when he pleaded with Cranmer for the life of *Joan Bocher* who was accused and condemned for heresy. Edward, broken-hearted exclaimed, "What my lord? Will ye have me send her quick to the devil, in all her error?" [3]

Suitable Matrimonial Alliance for the King

A union with Mary, the young queen of Scotland had originally been designed. After this did not materialize, some progress was made in a treaty with the royal family of France—the French king at that time in some respects approved the Reformation, but the English Protestants were much against such an alliance.

Latimer spoke with his accustomed clarity from the pulpit, advising the king "to choose one that is of God, that is of the household of faith and such an one as the king can find in his heart to love, and lead his life in pure and chaste espousage with. Let him choose a wife that fears God. Let him not choose a proud woman who is full only of rich treasures and worldly pomp." [4]

At one time an alliance was proposed with a daughter of the duke of Somerset, and at another time with *Lady Jane Grey. John ab Ulmis*, writing to *Bullinger* at one time respecting Lady Jane Grey,

[3] Mary M. Luke, *A Crown for Elizabeth,* Coward-McMann, Inc., N.Y., 1970.

[4] *Writings of Edward the Sixth*, 1831.

said, "A report becomes common and is current among the nobility that the king is to espouse this illustrious female. If that should come to pass, how happy the union! And how beneficial to the church may we expect it to prove." [5]

The King's Counsel to a Young Companion

Edward's maturity is clearly seen in the kind of counsel he gave to a close friend by the name of *Barnaby Fitzpatrick*. Edward and Barnaby were friends from childhood. In 1551, the youthful monarch sent Barnaby to Paris to attend the French court, that he might acquire some useful knowledge.

The great anxiety Edward felt for Barnaby's spiritual interests is revealed in a letter to Barnaby, dated December 20, 1551. He wrote, "We have received your letters of the 8th of the present month, whereby we understand how you are well entertained, for which we are right glad, and also how you have been asked once to go on pilgrimage [which apparently involved the celebration of the mass].

"For which cause we have thought good to advertise [inform, advise] you, that hereafter, if any such chance happen, you shall desire to leave to go to *Mr. Pickering* (English ambassador), or to Paris for your business. And if that will not serve, declare to some man of estimation with whom you are acquainted, that, as you are loth [loathe] to offend

[5] Ibid.

the French king because you have been so favorably used, so with safe conscience you cannot do any such thing, being brought up with me, and bound to obey my laws, also that you had a commandment from me to the contrary. Yet if you are vehemently procured, you may go, as waiting on the king, not as intending to the abuse, nor willingly seeing the ceremonies, and so you look not on the mass. But in the mean season, regard the holy Scripture, or some good Christian book, and give no reverence to the mass at all. Furthermore, remember when you may conveniently be absent from the court to tarry with *Sir William Pickering,* to be instructed by him how to use yourself." [6]

Further directions as to his conduct read, ". . . For women, as far as ye may, avoid their company. Yet, if the French King command you, you may sometimes dance. Else apply yourself to riding, shooting or tennis, with such honest games, not forgetting sometimes your learning, chiefly reading of the Scripture."

A disgruntled Barnaby replied, "Ye make me think the care ye take for me is more fatherly than friendly." [7]

It appears that there were some about the court who endeavored to turn the king from his laudable studies and pursuits to the usual light and frivolous pastimes of courts.

[6] Ibid.

[7] Alison Weir, *The Children of Henry VIII*, Ballantine Books, New York, 1996.

To the king, *Thomas Lever* said, "It is not unlike, but Your Majesty, with your Council, speak unto your nobles for provision now to be made for the poor people, ye shall find some, that setting afore your eyes the hardness of the matter, the tenderness of your years, and the wonderful charges that should be requisite, will move and counsel you to quiet yourself, to take your ease, yea, to take your pastime, in hawking, hunting and gaming."

And then turning to those who advised the king to engage in the "frivolous pastimes," Lever boldly addressed such, "Thou hast no taste nor savour how delicious God is unto a pure conscience in godly exercise of good works. But all that thou regardest and feelest is voluptuous pleasures in worldly vanities; and therefore thou dost not perceive, how that they which be endowed with a special grace of God, may find more pleasure and pastime in godly governance, to keep together and save simple men, than in hawking and hunting, to chase and kill wild beasts. Yea, a godly king shall find more pleasure in casting lots for Jonah, to try out offenders which trouble the ship of this commonwealth, than in casting dice at hazard, to allow and maintain by his example such things as should not be suffered in commonwealth. Yea, surely a good king shall take far more delight in edifying with comfort, and decking with good order, the congregation of his people, the church and house of God, the heavenly city of Jerusalem, than in building such houses as seem gay and gorgeous, and are indeed but vile earth, stones, timber and clay."

Turning to the king again, Lever continued, "Such like answer ought Your Majesty and all noblemen to make, if ye find any of your counsellors more carnal than spiritual, more worldly than godly."[8]

The Dowager Queen of Scots on her visit to the English court about this time, said that she found more wisdom and solid judgment in young King Edward than she would have looked for in any three princes that were in Europe.

Roger Ascham, Elizabeth's tutor, who was for a while involved in Edward's education, in writing to *Sturmius*, said that the nobles of England were never more attached to learning than now. He added, "Our illustrious king excels those of his own age, and even passes belief in understanding industry, perseverance and erudition. I did not learn this from the report of others, but from my own personal knowledge—and to witness it has afforded me much joy and blessing. I can say that the virtues appear to have taken up their abode in him."[9]

Addressing the Rebellions over the Uniformity Act

In December of 1549, Archbishop Cranmer and

[8] *Writings of Edward the Sixth*, 1831.
[9] Ibid.

his bishops publicly announced their rejection of the doctrine of transubstantiation and the *Act of Uniformity* on doctrine was passed by Parliament.

Many of the people did not understand it, and rebellions spread from Devonshire to Somerset and Cornwall and from Norfolk and Suffolk counties to the Midlands. The troops from London were reinforced with mercenaries from Germany and Italy. *John Dudley,* earl of Warwick, defeated the eastern rebels, killing three thousand five hundred in calvary charges. *Lord Russell* won victory in the west where four thousand peasants fell in the struggle for the mass and the *Six Articles* of Henry VIII, which advocated the Catholic doctrine. In this struggle Somerset vacillated and issued a general pardon which tended to bring further confusion.

Edward began taking part in the administration at this time and was present at the Council meetings when the cost of the wars was revealed. He was aware of the fact that the circulation of the Prayer Book which he personally encouraged was the cause of some of the rebellions, although when the First Prayer Book was published Edward was generally accepted by the people and was described as "the most noble ruler of his ship, even our most comfortable Noah."

Edward recognized the responsibility of the clergy to the people. "For as the good husbandman maketh the ground good and plentiful, so doth the true preacher with doctrine and example print and graft in the people's mind the Word of God." [10]

Cheke charged the Norfolk rebels, saying, "learn, learn to know this one point of religion . . . disobedience to His Majesty is an abominable sin . . . you have gathered together all the nasty vagabonds and idle loiterers to bear arms against His Majesty, whom all godly and good subjects will die for withal . . . . Shall not strangers think that the king's Majesty—in whose mind God hath powered so much hope for a child, and we may look for gifts in a man . . . . All England is despised by other countries . . . . The shame of your mischief will blemish the realm forever." [11]

The western rebels insisted on Roman Catholicism and said, "We will have the laws of our sovereign lord King Henry VIII concerning the Six Articles to be used again . . ." They did not seem to realize that they were being disobedient to the king who *now* reigned and that they flaunted the laws which he had approved.

Here Cheke rises and speaks and exhorts the rebels *as from Edward himself.* We may be certain that Edward fully understood and backed Cheke in what he was saying. Beginning with mild reproof, Edward (speaking through the mouth of Cheke) rises

[10] Mary M. Luke, *A Crown for Elizabeth,* 1970.
[11] *Writings of Edward the Sixth,* 1831.

to a strong expression of wrath:

"Ye would have them [the Articles] stand in force till our full age . . . If ye knew what ye spake, ye would never have uttered that notion, nor ever have given breath to such a thought. Be we of less authority for our age? Be we not your king now, as we shall be? . . . Ye must first know that, as a king, we have no difference of years or time, but as a natural man and creature of God, we have youth, and, by His sufferance, shall have age. We are your rightful king, your liege lord, your king anointed, your king crowned, the sovereign king of England, not by our age, but by God's ordinance . . . . We possess our crown, not by years, but by the blood and descent from our father King Henry VIII . . . and rule we will, because God hath willed it . . . . Thus far, ye see we have descended from our high majesty for love, to consider you in your base and simple ignorance, and have been content to send you instruction like a fatherly prince, who, of justice, might have sent you to your destruction . . . . We swear to you, by the living God, by Whom we reign, ye shall feel the power of the same God, in our sword, which how mighty it is, no subject knoweth; how puissant it is, no man can judge; how mortal it is, no English heart dare think. Repent yourselves, and take our mercy without delay." [12]

[12] Hester W. Chapman, *The Last Tudor King,* Ulverscroft, Leicester, 1958.

Leading up to the *Second Act of Uniformity* the Privy Council engaged in a lengthy debate on the subject of the *Eucharist,* which was opened by Somerset with an appeal for unity. Irked by his failure to win over *Bishop Thirlby,* who sided with the other Catholic bishops, Somerset said to Edward, "How much the Bishop of Westminister has deceived my expectations!" Edward replied, "Your expectations he might deceive but not mine." "How so?" Somerset asked. "I expected nothing else," Edward answered, "but that he, who has been so long a time with the Emperor should smell of the *Augsburg Interim* of Charles V the Emperor." [13] (The *Augsburg Interim* was adopted at the Diet of Augsburg under the leadership of Charles V, the Holy Roman Emperor and it became imperial law on June 30, 1548. Consisting of 26 articles, the Augsburg Interim reflected strongly the Roman Catholic viewpoint.)

Cranmer stated his position on the Sacrament thus: "spiritually He (that is Christ) is in them that *worthily* eat and drink of the same—but really, corporeally and carnally, He is only in Heaven." [14] The essense of Cranmer's position was to affirm a spiritual eucharistic presence granted by grace only to the elect believer, not to all who received bread and wine. In 1552 Parliament passed the second *Act of Uniformity* to which a new Prayer Book was annexed

[13] Ibid.

[14] *Writings of Edward the Sixth,* 1831.

and which declared the revision to be the only permissible liturgy in the realm. The third and final stage was the eucharistic discussion in the long-delayed doctrinal statement of the Edwardian Church, the *Forty-Two Articles,* published only a few weeks before Edward's death.

Edward's Treatise
Against the Primacy of the Pope

We will now examine Edward's great literary work which reveals his true greatness as a Bible scholar and a staunch believer in all the major tenets of the Protestant faith. Between December 1548 and March 1549, the king wrote his great *Treatise Against the Primacy of the Pope.* It is truly a remarkable production for a boy, less than twelve, even by modern standards. He takes the Scriptures which the Roman Catholics advance for the supremacy of the pope, and one by one he shows the errors of Rome and endeavors to show their true meaning.

Some of these are difficult passages to interpret and few Bible scholars of our day could improve on what Edward has done. Fewer still are the scholars who would have the courage to do what this young king was willing to do in identifying the pope of Rome for what he really was. Is it not true that the beliefs and teachings of Roman Catholics are supposed to be handed down by the "infallible" popes?

In this obscure composition the young king proves that Peter was never at Rome, that Peter never held authority over the other Apostles, that the early bishops of Rome itself rejected the idea of a pope and that the first pope was not "created" until five centuries later.

When *John Calvin* and *Henry Bullinger,* leading Reformers on the Continent at that time, first received a copy of Edward's Treatise, they found no fault with it.

Let us look at an enlightening paragraph or two where Edward interprets the "keys" of which our Lord spoke (Matt. 16:19) as meaning the proclamation of the true Gospel.

Edward wrote: "We see therefore, that the Gospel revealed in the holy Scriptures is the only gate to the kingdom of God.

"St. Paul says in Rom. 10:13-17: 'Whosoever shall call upon the name of the Lord, shall be saved. How then shall they call on Him in whom they have not believed? And how shall they believe in Him of whom they have not heard? And how shall they hear without a preacher?' Then he declared, 'So then faith cometh by hearing, and hearing by the word of God.' And in the fourth chapter to the Romans, he saith, 'But to him that worketh not, but believeth on Him that justifieth the ungodly, his faith is counted for righteousness' (4:5). Moreover, we will prove that the preaching of the Gospel is the key of heaven. Paul affirms that, 'Whoever calls upon the name of the Lord, shall be saved'; that the preaching of the Gospel is the door to heaven—the preaching of the Gospel is the way of salvation.

"Again, Paul affirms that faith justifies, and that the preaching of the Gospel brings faith. It follows that the preaching of the true word of God is the door to heaven and brings about justification. Like as ground which is sowed may produce fruit, if the seed be planted. So, if the word of God be sowed in the hearts of honest people, or such as have a zeal for truth, it will confirm them in all goodness; but if any be obstinate and perverse, they cannot attribute the fault unto the holy Scriptures. The fault is really in themselves.

"Therefore we ought to do our utmost to cause the Gospel to be preached throughout all the world; as it is written, 'All power is given unto Me in heaven and in earth: go ye therefore, and teach all nations, baptizing them in My name' (Matt. 28:18; Mk. 16:15, 16; Lu. 24:47, 48).

"Since then it is proved that the 'keys' to heaven represent the authority of preaching; and that the authority of preaching was given to *all* the apostles, therefore, according to that text, no greater authority was given to Peter than to the other disciples. St. Paul says, that he himself was not a 'whit behind the very chiefest apostles' (2 Cor. 11:5)."

Edward dedicated his treatise to Somerset, his uncle, but we find there is no record of his uncle's reaction. This treatise was first printed in May of 1553, but we have virtually no information regarding its acceptance among the people in England. We do find that it was highly regarded among the reformers on the continent. After Somerset's fall, Edward's lengthy treatise was printed and bound in gilded quarto decorated with the Royal Arms. We can assume that the king and the Council, of which Northumberland was the undisputed leader, were launching out on an anti-papal crusade.

You will find the complete treatise within the compass of this book. Edward does not have a single word concerning it in his *Chronicles* which he began to write about this time.

This remarkable study by the English monarch seems to establish him definitely as the King of England *whose eyes God had opened* and for whom Tyndale had prayed. His understanding of the Scriptures and all his actions place him into a position with respect to the advancement of Protestantism as being above all other monarchs during those dark centuries.

The Reformation, or Revolution, as some historians call it, advanced steadily from the commencement of the reign of Edward VI. That much remained imperfect may readily be admitted, but at no previous period of English history was true Christianity more generally prevalent than in the reign of King Edward VI, although it is true that many of the people at first objected to the Reformation doctrines.

King Edward was scarcely twelve years old, when he wrote the lengthy article "Against the Primacy of the Pope." We stand amazed, and then we remember how Jesus was found in the temple, "sitting in the midst of the doctors, both hearing them and asking them questions. And all that heard Him were astonished at His understanding and answers" (Lu. 2:46, 47). When questioned by His mother, He replied firmly, "Know you not that I must be about my Father's business?" (Lu. 2:48, 49). Jesus was then twelve years of age. This was the age of Edward when he composed his treatise.

8

The King Manipulated by the Protectors

Following the rebellions, a crisis developed between Somerset and the Council. On October 5, 1549, Edward summoned "all his loving subjects" to come to Hampton Court to defend him and the Protector. On October 6, Somerset dispatched a messenger to Warwick demanding to know what was going on. The messenger did not return, and Somerset learned that the "London lords," which included the Council members, were on the march to Hampton Court.

Somerset decided that, since his allies in London were falling away, he should awaken the king and head for Windsor Castle. He had him dressed and escorted down to the courtyard, which was lit by flares and filled with the Protector's troops. "At his uncle's behest, the king raised the toy dagger, brilliant with jewels, given him by his father, and enjoined the soldiers to follow him against his enemies and all traitors. With one voice they responded: 'God save Your Grace! We would all die for you!' " [1]

Somerset tried to hurry things along, and shortly thereafter they galloped into the night and reached Windsor Castle by daylight. Soon after, Cranmer, Paget and *Sir Thomas Smith* arrived with three hundred armed men. Somerset moved as if he expected civil war would follow. "Watch and ward," the king tells us, was kept every night.

On the 7th of October messengers galloped between Windsor and London. Cranmer and Paget advised Somerset to see the Lords and the Council and come to some agreement rather than risk civil war. On October 8, the king sent a letter to the Council asking that the quarrel should be ended. Edward confided to Paget that he felt as if he were in a prison. Paget noticed also that Edward had a bad cold, and although the king was loyal to his uncle, it was clear that he was deeply concerned about the turn of events.

Then came the demand from the Council that Somerset surrrender his office of Protector peacefully. Somerset did so and submitted to the formality of an arrest. Three days later Somerset and his Duchess were escorted from Windsor to the Tower

---

[1] Alison Weir, *The Children of Henry VIII,* Ballantine Books, New York, 1996.

of London where he was interrogated by his former colleagues. He confessed to a list of articles which were laid against him.

Edward expressed tearful concern for his uncle, saying, "What evil has he done, that he should be arrested? The Duke never did any harm. As he went to the Tower of his own will, it is a sign that he be not guilty."[2]

At the next Council meeting Edward asked that Somerset's life be spared. This was the occasion when the grandiose Warwick, soon to become the Duke of Northumberland, thought it judicious and good for the sake of his own future plans to be generous. He arose and said ever so graciously, "My lords, we must return good for evil. And as it is the king's will that the Duke should be pardoned, and it is the first matter he hath asked of us, we ought to accede to His Grace's wish."[3]

Six months after his arrest, Somerset was restored to the Council, but not as Protector. Somerset's authority and title were wrongly usurped, and the condescending Northumberland rose to the top. The phenomenal, wicked cleverness with which Northumberland pursued his two chief objectives is noteworthy, though shameful. First he set out to gain the friendship and the confidence of the king, second the execution of Somerset.

[2] Hester W. Chapman, *The Last Tudor King*, Ulverscroft, Leicester, 1958.

[3] Ibid.

Although in the reorganization of the Council, Northumberland took fourth place officially, yet he set himself up as Lord President of the Council and the ruler of England. The office of Lord Protector was allowed to lapse. He made it his business always to ingratiate himself with the king, allowing Edward more money and letting him have more voice in matters of state.

In October 1551, Somerset was again arrested and sent to the tower, and Northumberland soon took up the matter against him. Upon the insistence of Edward an open trial for Somerset was arranged. They debated for six hours. False witnesses against Somerset were brought in by Northumberland. These testified that Somerset planned the assassination of Northumberland and other Council members. Thus the fate of Somerset was sealed.

Edward himself did not fully grasp what had happened, and stated in his *Chronicle* that Somerset "seemed to confess he went about their death." On January 18, 1552, Edward drew up some notes for the Council meeting. One read as follows, "The matter for the Duke of Somerset's confederates to be considered, as appertaineth to our surety and quietness of our realm, that by their punishment example may be showed to others."

This he signed on January 18, 1552. Between the 18th and 19th of January this memorandum was partially erased, and so interlined that it read as follows:

". . . that by their punishment *and execution according to the laws*, example should be showed to others." Later examination indicated that the extra words were actually forged, although this could not be clearly established. Three days passed and Northumberland in his "angelic" approach asked the king about the matter relating to his uncle. Edward was overwhelmed, and although he did not clearly understand what had happened, said, "Let the law take its course."[4]

It might be well to insert at this point what happened at another Council meeting where the king was asked for a reprieve for one of the prisoners. One author states that Edward "very deliberately" asked, "How is this, my lords? There was no one to beg for mercy for my uncle—and for this man you all come."[5]

The day of January 22nd dawned. Somerset appeared serene and stately. As they rode to the scaffold, *Sir Thomas Arundel* said to another nobleman: "His blood will make my lord Northumberland's pillow uneasy."

Standing high above the people, Somerset leaned forward and delivered a timeless, stirring valedictory, solid in his faith in Christ: "I have endured the hate of great persons—so much the more dangerous because unjust. I have incurred displeasure from inferiors, for giving way to the faults of others—and

[4] Ibid.
[5] Ibid.

84

now, being constantly resolved, I neither fear to die, nor desire to live. Let us now join in prayer to the Lord for the preservation of the King's Majesty, to whose Grace I have always been a faithful, true and most loving subject, desirous always of his most prosperous success in all his affairs, and ever glad of the helping forward of the commonwealth of this realm.

"If there are any that have been offended and injured by me," the Duke resumed, "I most humbly ask him forgiveness—but especially Almighty God, Whom throughout my life I have most grievously offended. And all others, whatsoever they be," he added emphatically, "I do with my whole heart forgive them." Shouts and curses against Northumberland and the Council arose. Somerset called for silence, saying: "I once again require you, dearly beloved in the Lord, that you all keep yourselves quiet and still, lest by your tumult you should trouble me. For albeit the spirit be ready and willing, the flesh is frail and wavering—and through your quietness I shall be much more quiet.

"I desire you all to bear me witness that I die here in the faith of Jesus Christ—desiring you all to help me with your prayers, that I may persevere constant in the same." [6]

He knelt to pray, "Lord Jesu, receive my soul."

And the axe fell!

[6] Ibid.

85

Although Somerset was not free from failure in that he entered into some wars rashly, followed his own opinions, doing things by his own authority and possibly enriching himself from the king's treasury, yet such failures hardly warranted his execution. It was in these sad events that the young monarch was manipulated by Northumberland and drawn into a trap where he signed Somerset's death warrant. Although the evil Northumberland did his utmost to draw the king into his net and line him up against Somerset, the king later blamed himself for failing to save his uncle.

Edward's self-examination follows:

"Upon the death of the Duke [Somerset] albeit the King gave no token of any distempered passion, as takeinge it not agreeable to maiestie openly to declare himself, and the Lords had laboured with much variety of sports, to dispell any dampy thoughts, which the remembrance of his uncle might rayse, yet upon speech of him hee would often sigh and lett fall teares. Sometymes holdinge opinion that his Unckle had done nothinge, or if hee had, it was very small and proceeded rather from his wife than from himselfe, and where then said hee was the good nature of a Nephewe? Where was the clemency of a Prince? Ah how unfortunate have I beene to those of my bloud, my mother I slewe at my birth, and since then have made away two of

her brothers, and happily to make away for others against myselfe, was it ever known before that a King's Unckle, a lord Protector, one whose fortunes had much advanced the Honour of the realme, did lose his head for felony; for a felony neither cleere in Law, and in fact weakley proved. Alas so how falsely have I been abused? how weakly carried? howe little was I master of myne own Judgment, that both his death and the envy thereof must be layd upon me." [7]

The King's remorse and acceptance of moral responsibility speak well for his conscientious attitude and character though not wholly excusing him from failure. He was deluded by the machinations of his elders, particularly those of Northumberland, and his contrite confession reveals his humility and submission to God.

Northumberland lived long enough to do more evil—especially to the King of England, but nineteen months after the fall of Somerset, waiting to be executed on the very same spot, solemnly announced within moments of his death, that the Duke of Somerset had been falsely accused in evidence set out and provided by himself and his cohorts. Northumberland was perhaps, the most subtle intriguer in England's history.

---

[7] Beer, ed., *Life and Raigne of Edward the Sixth*, quoted by Jennifer Loach in *Edward VI*, 1999.

Ring Edward and His Sisters

From his very infancy, Edward was deeply loved by his sisters. They doted over him. Mary, who loved children, showered him with attention and with gifts. Edward grew fond of his older sister and in time responded with gifts. Edward promised Mary never to betray any of her secrets.

When Edward embraced the true faith, which the Protestants taught, the gulf between him and Mary began to widen. For a long time they avoided the subject of religion when they met. Edward knew full well that Mary cherished the hope that when he became older he would return to the faith of his infancy.

In 1543, *Katherine Parr*, Henry's sixth wife, re-united Henry with all his children and gave them their first experience of a quiet family life. Katherine Parr leaned definitely toward the Protestant faith, but she refrained from pressing her views, nor did she inter-fere with Mary's strong loyalty to Catholicism.

Edward and his sisters became fond of her and enjoyed being together as a family.

Edward was closer to Elizabeth probably because she was only four years older than he was. His letters to her were always warm and loving. "Change of place did not vex me so much," he wrote Elizabeth, "dearest sister, as your going from me. Now there can be nothing pleasanter than a letter from you. It is some comfort in my grief that my chamberlain tells me I may hope to visit you very soon if nothing happens to either of us in the meantime. Farewell, dearest sister." [1]

The thing that probably bound these two so closely together was the fact that they realized that they both lost their mothers through the difficult strokes of providence. When she was six, Elizabeth made Edward a cambric shirt for a New Year's gift. As they grew older they frequently corresponded— mostly in Latin—and encouraged one another to excel intellectually. After Edward became king, their letters were marked by a new formality. Court etiquette prevented their former intimacy, yet the bonds of affection continued.

The ordinary people lacked instruction in the matter of worship. Cranmer was aware of this and in March of 1548 he had published an *Order of Communion* containing instructions in English for

---

[1] Alison Weir, *The Children of Henry VIII*, Ballantine Books, New York, 1996.

inclusion in the Latin mass. Towards the end of 1548 Cranmer had a panel of some thirteen theologians meeting at Windsor to compose a new liturgy. This was incorporated into the *Book of Common Prayer* and was approved by Parliament in January of 1549. This became the *Act of Uniformity* which imposed punishment for those who objected or declined to use it. The 1549 Prayer Book sought to retain the sympathy of Roman Catholics while satisfying the Reformers. However, much confusion prevailed.

But it was generally understood that any priest caught celebrating mass according to the old Roman Catholic form would be guilty of a crime. For this he could first be fined, and then, if he continued the abuse, he would be imprisoned.

Mary's adherence to the Roman Catholic religion and having the mass sung in her household began to divide her from her siblings.

Mary categorically refused to listen, and declared that she would not conform to the new Act and would never use the *Book of Common Prayer*. The Council wrote her a stern letter, advising her to "be conformable and obedient to the observation of His Majesty's laws to give orders that mass should no more be used in her house, and that she embrace and cause to be celebrated the Communion."

Mary responded with indignation, "I have offended no law, unless it be a late law of your own making for the altering of matters of religion, which, in my conscience, is not worthy to have the name of law. When His Majesty comes of age he shall find me his good and obedient subject in this, as in every other matter, but until then I have no intention of changing the practices dictated by my conscience."[2]

The Holy Roman Emperor, *Charles V,* Mary's cousin, threatened England if they disallowed mass for the princess. At this some of the Council members suggested that Edward's sister's disobedience with respect to the mass be tolerated in order to pacify the Emperor.

Edward inquired, "Is it lawful by Scripture to sanction idolatry?"

A bishop replied, "There were good kings [in biblical times], Your Majesty, who allowed the hill altars, and yet were called good."

"We must follow the example of good men when they have done well," the young king declared. "We do not follow them in evil. David was good but David seduced Bathsheba and murdered Uriah. We are not to imitate David in such deeds as these. Is there no better Scripture?"[3]

The bishops were silenced.

"I am sorry for the realm, then, and sorry for the danger that will come of it," Edward concluded.

Cranmer, coming out of the Council Chamber

[2] Ibid.
[3] Ibid.

91

and finding Cheke in one of the ante-rooms, took him by the hand and said: "Ah! Master Cheke, you may be glad all the days of your life that you have such a scholar, for he [Edward] hath more divinity in his little finger than we have in our whole bodies."[4]

At Edward's insistence, the Council composed a letter to Mary condemning her "wayward misunderstanding," to which Edward added some sentences in his own hand. He denied that she had ever been granted official permission to continue attending mass in her house, and that her offence was the more heinous because she was setting a terrible example for his people. The letter went on:

"It is a scandalous thing that so high a personage should deny our sovereignty. That our sister should be less to us than any of our other subjects is an unnatural example. In our state, it shall miscontent us to permit you, so great a subject, not to permit our laws. Your nearness to us in blood, your greatness in estate, the condition of this time, maketh your fault the greater. To teach you and instruct you we will give order and so procure you to do your duty willingly, that you shall perceive you are not used merely as a subject, and only commanded but as a daughter, a scholar and a sister, taught, instructed and persuaded. You shall err in many points, such as our father and yours would

[4] Hester W. Chapman, *The Last Tudor King*, Ulverscroft, Leicester, 1958.

not have suffered, whatsoever you say of the standing still of things as they were left by him. Truly, sister, I will not say more and worse things, because my duty would compel me to use harsher and angrier words. But this I will say with certain intention, that I will see my laws strictly obeyed, and those who break them shall be watched and denounced." [5]

Mary felt devastated to receive this stinging admonition. It ended her hopes that Edward would return to the Catholic faith when he reached his majority. She answered him, saying, "Your Majesty hath far more knowledge and greater gifts than other of your years, yet it is not possible that Your Highness can at these years be a judge in matters of religion." He would know better, she went on to say, when he reached "ripe and fuller years." [6]

Mary Summoned to Appear at Court

On the 15th of March, 1551, Mary arrived in London attended by fifty knights and gentlemen in velvet coats and chains of gold before her, and after her fourscore ladies and gentlemen, everyone wearing a pair of black beads. All carried their rosaries thus proclaiming themselves supporters of Mary in her defiance as a Catholic. The people ran five or six miles out of town and were so happy to see her.

[5] Alison Weir, *The Children of Henry VIII*, 1996.
[6] Ibid.

Four hundred people followed her into the city.

Two days later she went in procession to Whitehall where the king was in residence and where all the members of the Council had assembled. Mary fell on her knees. Edward raised her, kissed her. He then led her alone into an adjoining chamber followed by the Council members. For the next two hours she defended her views amidst heated arguments. At the sight of her profuse tears, Edward wept also, saying, he intended no harm to her, but the religious gulf between them was so great that there seemed to be no meeting ground. Finally she appealed to the king begging him to allow the matter to rest until he was of an age to reach a mature judgment in matters of religion.

Edward replied with conviction that Mary too might have something to learn—no one was too old for that. He expressed concern about her conduct and that her example was breeding unrest and trouble in the realm. He then informed her that his Master of Horse, *Sir Anthony Browne*, had just been incarcerated for twice attending mass at her house. Unless he saw a change in her, he told Mary, he would not be able to bear it. Mary answered that her faith she would not change, nor dissemble her opinion with contrary doings.

"There are two things only, body and soul," she said. "Although my soul belongs to God, I offer my body to the king's service; might it please him to take away my life rather than my old religion."[7] Edward answered her gently and assured her that he "had no desire for such a sacrifice." The king told her to go home whilst he discussed her case with the Council.

After she left, the Council engaged in heated debate. Many were advocating her immediate arrest and the Tower. For the time being Mary was exempt from persecution but her priests were not. On the 23rd of April the priests—*Rochester, Englefield* and *Waldegrave* along with *Dr. Mallet*—were committed to the Tower, and Mary was told that time had now expired and she was required to obey the king's laws as did everyone else.

For two years her household had no mass. The troubled Mary had to send away her chaplains for their own sakes. She herself had mass but behind locked doors and in fear and trembling. Only three of her servants knew that in their midst was a priest in disguise who could give to their mistress what she could not live without—the mass. These are some of the details of the king's unhappy relationship with his sister Mary.

Edward and Elizabeth

Edward asked Elizabeth for a portrait after Christmas, which she immediately sent to him with a gracious letter: "I shall most humbly beseech Your

[7] Hester W. Chapman, *The Last Tudor King,* 1958.

Majesty, that when you look on my picture, you will witsafe to think that as you have not the outward show of my body, so my inward mind wisheth that the body itself were oftener in your presence."[8]

After the ordeal with his sister Mary, Edward had the joy of meeting with his sister Elizabeth who had been estranged from the king and the Council by the Thomas Seymour flirtations, in which she was an innocent party.

The Council invited her to the Royal Palace. After Christmas she came and joyfully rode on horseback through London to St. James Palace with an entourage of lords, knights, gentlemen and about two hundred ladies. In contrast to Mary, this sister was indisputably an advocate of her brother's faith and convictions.

Elizabeth's triumph is well reflected in the effusive letter she wrote Edward upon her return to her abode: "No more frequent or plainer proofs can be given of your love for me. Oh most serene and illustrious king, than those of late when I enjoyed the treat of your most delightful society. This when I call to mind (and I daily do so) I seem, as it were, still enjoying the courtesy of your conversations. And farther, when those your countless favors to me come to mind, with which you received me on my arrival and with which you dismissed me on my departure, I cannot easily express . . ."[9]

[8] Alison Weir, *The Children of Henry VIII*, 1996.

[9] Mary M. Luke, *A Crown for Elizabeth*, Coward-McMann, Inc., N. Y., 1970.

In March, Elizabeth again visited the king, attended by a large retinue, and it was a comfort to both of them.

Roger Ascham was back in the service of Elizabeth, not as a tutor, but as a friend. In a letter to *Johann Sturm,* rector of the Protestant University of Strasbourg, he said, "Lady Elizabeth shines like a star. So much solidity of understanding, so much courtesy united with dignity, have never been observed at so early an age. She has the most ardent love of the true religion and of the best kind of literature. No apprehension can be quicker than hers, no memory more retentive." [10]

Edward and His Sisters

Edward's affection for his sisters survived his conflicts with them over religion, politics or scandal. This is evidenced in his correspondence with them and in his continued invitations to visit him at court. Their affection for him was also evident though his Councillors, Warwick in particular, conspired to keep them apart so as not to allow them any influence over the king or his policies.

In 1552, when Edward had been ill after Yule, Mary passed through London on her way to visit him at Westminster. She left a day or two after her arrival, and the Candelmas festivities they were to share did not take place. Again in February, the

[10] Alison Weir, *The Children of Henry VIII,* 1996.

month of her thirty-seventh birthday, Mary rode along Fleet Street on her way to visit Edward. She found herself accompanied by the wives of those with the highest positions in the realm, while at the gates of the palace their husbands, headed by the Duke of Northumberland himself, waited to greet her. She waited for three days before Edward was well enough to see her and then, there could be no intimacy between brother and sister for the short time she was there, because his doctors were present throughout and he had difficulty in breathing.

It was decided that all Edward needed was country air. Before leaving London for Greenwich in April, he gave Mary a handsome table-cut diamond, a gift that carried its own portent in the eyes of her advisors. She waited in vain in the manor of Beaulieu and made fruitless efforts to visit him.

Meanwhile Elizabeth, now twenty, waited at Hatfield. This was her favorite place, where she had spent much of her youth, and the little brother who had shared so many hours with her there had given it to her on that memorable visit to him only two short years ago. Like her sister, she now made every effort to see him, for rumors were rampant regarding his health, and like Mary her every attempt was foiled, nor were any of her letters allowed to reach him.

Before April was out, Edward was no longer able to walk in the gardens, and his doctors were continually in attendance. He began to know his time was short and his thoughts turned to the succession, on the question of who would reign when he was gone.

Despite his affection for his sisters, he could not find it in his heart to entrust either of them with what God had entrusted to him. How could he leave his realm, his temporal kingdom, in the hands of one who would lead it back into idolatry? Even Elizabeth, who professed to be a Protestant, would likely marry a foreign prince, a Catholic, who would undo all the good he, Edward, had done in advancing the kingdom in the true faith. This foreign prince could abolish all the realm's ancient rights until he extinguished the very name of England. Thus either sister could wreck the Reformation which their father had begun and which he, Edward, with God's grace had brought to such goodly fruition. Yes, despite his affection for them, despite his father's will for the succession, he felt the need to be guided by what was best for the realm and the perpetuation of the Protestant and true faith.

⌁ *10* ⌁

𝕽ing 𝕰dward and 𝕻roteftantf from the 𝕮ontinent

King Edward VI, the valiant boy-king and the thunderbolt and terror of the papists, encouraged and helped Protestant leaders on the continent to come to England. The *Augsburg Interim*, prepared under the influence of Emperor Charles V, primarily reflected the Catholic viewpoint, and was proclaimed in May of 1548. Many of the leading Reformers felt the pressure and emigrated to England.

Martin Bucer, (1491-1551), an early associate of *Martin Luther* and a renowned preacher at Strasbourg, sought to bring about a doctrinal compromise between the followers of *Zwingli* in Switzerland and Luther in Germany. *Peter Martyr* who was already in England added his voice to that of Cranmer in encouraging Bucer to come. Bucer was forthwith appointed Regius Professor of Divinity at Cambridge. He expressed his joy at being in

England "where the Bible may now be freely read and where the public faith will be founded on its precepts. Already it may be said that there is not one realm that hath more well learned and godly men in authority, nor none wherein bishops, excel in so much of doctrine and purity of life." [1]

The young king himself was highly solicitous for the welfare and comfort of these learned refugees who were a good deal inconvenienced by some manners and customs in England. While Bucer was still living, the king heard that he suffered in health for want of a heated room such as he was accustomed to in Germany. The king wasted no time in sending Bucer twenty pounds to defray the expense of constructing a stove before winter. Bucer in return wrote a book as a New Year's gift for the king. It was entitled, "Concerning the Kingdom of Christ." It contained much information on the subject of the Reformation and probably entailed a general discussion on that subject on which the king himself had written. After Bucer's departure to be with the Lord, the king showed kind attention to the interests of his widow.

When the city of Strasbourg urgently requested the return of Peter Martyr, the king did all he could to keep Martyr from leaving.

Bernardino Ochino (1487-1564), one of the

[1] *Writings of Edward the Sixth*, The Religious Tract Society, London, 1831.

greatest preachers of the Reformation, finally joined Martyr for the journey to England. He remained as an honored guest in Cranmer's household for four months before being appointed a prebendary (a cleric receiving a stipend from the Cathedral) of Canterbury. "Within a month Ochino had been authorized to set up an independent congregation in London catering mainly to Italians, but also for any other 'strangers' (that is resident aliens) who might choose to attend. It was never large, but it has the distinction of being the first officially recognized foreign Protestant congregation in England, anticipating by three years the much better known 'Stranger Church' led by Polish evangelical *Jan Laski.* "[2] The inauguration of Ochino's congregation in January 1548 was an extraordinary affair in which *Bishop Bonner* (not a Protestant) participated as a result of some shrewd maneuvering by Cranmer.

This famous Italian preacher spent much of his time in writing. The Princess Elizabeth translated one of his books from Italian into English.

Paul Fagius left for England on March 24, 1549. His judgment was that the English Church left little to be desired. Fagius had no more than sketched out his lectures on Isaiah when death overtook him. He was succeeded at Cambridge by *Emmanuel Tremellius* (1510-1580) an Italian

[2] Diarmaid MacCulloch, *The Boy King, Edward VI and the Protestant Reformation,* Palgrave Publishers, New York, 2001.

Jew who had been converted in 1540. He gained a considerable reputation at Cambridge for his Hebrew scholarship. He fled from England on the accession of Mary.

Peter Alexander of Arles, on Cranmer's suggestion made a careful study of the views of the early fathers on all the doctrinal issues in dispute. Drawn from France were *John Belmain* and *Valerand Poulain*. Another figure of considerable stature was *John Utenhove*, a native of Ghent, who helped with the settling and organization of the hundreds of lay refugees now streaming into England.

Of a somewhat greater intellectual stature than those already mentioned was *Francis Dryander*. Born in Spain in 1520, he was sent to the Netherlands. In 1541 he removed to Wittenberg where he studied under Melanchthon and translated the New Testament from Greek to Spanish. Somewhat restless in nature, he travelled to Switzerland and then later settled in Strasbourg.

Cranmer offered every inducement to get *Melanchthon* to England whereby doctrinal unity could be achieved. His duties, however, kept him from leaving Germany.

The inimitable *John ab Ulmis* came to England with a letter from kindly *Henry Bullinger*. He spent much of his time in London and from there he urged his friends at home to come to this land where the truth of the Gospel was flourishing. He wrote his friend Bullinger from Oxford in 1548. He said, "England is adorned and enlightened by the word of God, and the number of the faithful increases largely every day. The mass, so dear to the papists, begins to give way; in many places it is already dismissed and condemned by divine authority. Images are extirpated throughout the land, nor does the least spark remain which can afford hope to the papists, or give them an occasion for confirming their errors respecting idols, or an opportunity of drawing aside the people from our Saviour. The marriage of the clergy is allowed and sanctioned by royal approbation.

"Peter Martyr has demonstrated to general satisfaction, from the Scriptures, and the writings of orthodox divines, that purgatory is only a cross to which we have been hitherto subjected. The same result has taken place respecting the Eucharist, or the holy supper of the Lord—that it is a commemoration of Christ and a solemn showing forth of his death, not a sacrifice." [3]

Such reports by foreigners visiting England encouraged the king who at eleven years of age was seriously attending to the duties of the kingly office. In a paragraph concerning His Majesty's outward affairs which appears to be from the pen of the king, we read, "Albeit that our quarrel is in God, and God our quarrel, who never faileth them that trust in Him;

[3] *Writings of Edward the Sixth*, 1831.

yet forasmuch as wickedness reigneth in the midst of us, like as we should not mistrust the goodness of God, so ought we neither to neglect that policy which may help us to avoid the like captivity, that for wickedness happened to the elect people of Israel."

It appears that this young king always remembered the word of the Lord: "By Me kings reign" (Prov. 8:15).

Henry Bullinger, a leading Reformer in Switzerland and a close friend of *John Calvin*, addressed the king in a preface to a series of sermons, which at once showed his own faithfulness to the word of God and his opinion of the Christian principles of the English monarch. He urged him "to hold it as an undoubted truth that true prosperity was to be obtained by him no other way, than by submitting himself and his whole kingdom to Christ, the highest Prince, and by framing all matters of religion and justice throughout his dominions according to the truth of God's word; not stirring one inch from that rule; propagating the kingdom of Christ, and trampling upon that of Antichrist, as he had so happily begun." [4]

---

[4] Ibid.

105

≈ II ≈

The Last Days and Legacy of King Edward VI

It was one of the Protestants from a foreign country that after visiting the young king, said that he was "an angel in a human body." Of course he was a mere human being; it was his eyes that always made him look angelic.

In the year 1552, the king was attacked by measles and the small-pox. From the effects of these maladies he never fully recovered.

It so happened that *Girolamo Cardano*, the celebrated Italian doctor and mathematician, had just come back from a visit to the Bishop of St. Andrews, whom he had cured of asthma. In London he stayed with Cheke and was asked to give his diagnosis of Edward. Cardano disliked all the king's ministers, Northumberland especially, finding them hard and unscrupulous. He was reluctant to give his real opinion, but stated that "the king could live till the age of fifty-five."

It may have been about this time that Edward wrote in the fly-leaf of Palearion's *Benefit of Christ's Death*, "Live to die, and die to live again."

In April of 1553, Edward VI left his capital for the last time. He was taken from the Palace of Westminster to Greenwich Palace in a state barge. The flags were flown as for some triumphant entry.

Edward was very ill and clung to *Henry Sidney* and Cheke; he would hardly allow Sidney to leave his room. "I am glad to die," Cheke heard him whisper. Then a long prayer was heard and written out, and, long afterwards, it was published. "Lord God," they heard him say, "deliver me out of this miserable and wretched life, and take me amongst Thy chosen; howbeit, not my will but Thine be done. Lord, I commit my spirit to Thee. O! Lord, Thou knowest how happy it were for me to be with Thee: yet, for Thy chosen's sake, send me life and health, that I may truly serve Thee. O! Lord God, bless Thy people and save Thine inheritance. O! my Lord God, defend this realm from papistry, and maintain Thy true religion, that I and my people may praise Thy holy name, for Thy Son Jesus Christ's sake. Amen." [1]

Perhaps it was Cheke who said, that it would have been a great mercy if Edward had departed to

[1] *Writings of Edward the Sixth*, The Religious Tract Society, London, 1831.

be with the Lord following this prayer.

The king's serious illness gave rise to ambitious projects on the part of the bold and unprincipled duke of Northumberland. He resolved to secure the crown if possible to his own family. His designs were greatly enhanced by the king's sincere attachment to the truth of the Protestant cause. Edward was deeply apprehensive, that a devoted papist like his sister Mary might succeed to the throne. And it was precisely for this reason that he fell into the trap that Northumberland had been preparing for him over a period of time.

On May 25, 1553, *Lady Jane Grey* was married to *Guilford Dudley* (Northumberland's son). She hated Guilford but her obedience was enforced by a beating from her own father. Guilford made no secret of his dislike for his bride, but the schemes of his father, the evil Northumberland, must move on!

It now only remained to get Edward's agreement in rescinding the late king's will, and making one in favor of Lady Jane Grey. Northumberland stayed alone with Edward until he hammered into his vulnerable mind the necessity of declaring both Mary and Elizabeth as illegitimate and draw up the new device for the succession.

John Knox, the reformer of Scotland, who seemed to understand the evil work of Northumberland, in a sermon at the court boldly reproved the ill-conduct of the duke of Northumberland

and the marquess of Winchester, even to their faces. Instead of incurring royal displeasure by such a message, a pastorate in the city of London was offered him. He refused the offer, but he was still retained as one of the six itinerating preachers appointed by the king.

On June 10th, the doctors said that His Majesty could not live for more than three days. Here is where Northumberland moved in. He ignored the verdict of Wendy, Owen and Butts, who had been in charge of Edward's health since his birth, and turned them out of Edward's sick room. He called for the opinion of two people: his own doctor, who was a professor of medicine at Oxford, and a female "quack" whose name has been withheld. The woman stated that she was perfectly capable of curing His Majesty provided she was given a free hand. Northumberland consented and she began her duty by giving Edward a dose of what she called, "restringents," and which seem to have included arsenic. The immediate effect was a definite physical rally, but the devil was at work through the schemes of Northumberland.

Edward became stronger than he had been for some time. He signed the "device for the succession," and now he was making sure that all the Council members signed it. The Lord Chief Justice, *Sir Edward Montague* said that what His Majesty required was illegal and could not be drawn up without an Act of Parliament. Montague and his associates agreed that the king's device was illegal, and to sign it would be a criminal act. Northumberland became violent, and Montague felt that immediate arrest would be the next step. Edward, unfortunately, spoke very angrily to Montague and the others and insisted that they sign it. They did so under the condition His Majesty would grant them a licence under the Great Seal— and a pardon for having signed the device.

Still the most important of all signatures— Cranmer's—was missing. This was Cranmer's most difficult task. Edward was determined not to die until the Archbishop had signed the document. Cranmer asked if he might consult with the judges before making up his mind; he never forgot the affectionate look with which dear Edward granted his request. Northumberland bullied him. Finally, Cranmer consented in order that the person he most loved in the world might die in peace.

Edward was now dying from the poison that had at first stimulated him. He had eaten nothing since June 11th. His legs and arms swelled, his skin darkened, his nails and his hair fell off, his fingers and toes became gangrenous. During the week of July 1st Northumberland dismissed his own doctor and recalled Edward's regular physicians. The quack disappeared, and whether she was murdered or not is not known. Northumberland now intended to kidnap and imprison the Princess Mary as soon as she reached London.

Henry Sidney took Edward in his arms holding him to his breast. The king was praying and Dr. Owen said: "We heard you speak to yourself—but what you said we do not know." Edward smiled. "I was praying to God," he said. There was a long silence; then he murmured, "I am faint . . ." and the dear child of God said quite plainly, "Lord, have mercy upon me—take my spirit." The doctors held him between them until he died. Unrest abounded throughout London and beyond. The two sisters were never informed of the king's condition. They became suspicious, however, and were on their way to London when the king died.

The King Departs to His Eternal Rest

"That incomparable young prince," as *Bishop Burnet* calls him, died on the 6th day of July, 1553, at the age of fifteen.

His ailments may have been cleared up by his regular doctors and attendants had not the "quack" moved in with her "ministrations" at the behest of the wicked Northumberland. Edward's desire to serve God and the people may have been prolonged for years. We do not know.

The saintly king departed amidst the maneuverings of an evil man and his associates. God had used Edward in a wonderful way in the land where spiritual darkness had so long prevailed. It was said of him by *Bishop Hooper*, "He died young but lived long, if life be action." *John Bale*, a distinguished Christian author of the day, tells that he had often observed the king at public prayers when the words, "O Lord, save Thy people" were repeated, joining most fervently with clasped hands and eyes lifted up to heaven.

The Funeral of King Edward VI

The funeral of this noble king was solemnized at Westminster Abbey on August 8, 1553. The night before the funeral, Queen Mary had commanded that "the funeral service should be said in her chapel in Latin as the custom was in Rome." But Archbishop Cranmer opposed this vigorously and insisted that as the king himself had been a zealous promoter of the Reformation, so his funeral service should be in English and according to the existing English law. He stoutly resisted the queen and himself performed all the offices of the burial and joined with it the solemnity of a communion. Although *Burnet* states that "*Day,* bishop of Chichester, preached the funeral sermon for King Edward," the stronger likelihood is that Cranmer himself did it.

Dear Cranmer, as may well be imagined, presided at that service with heart sorrow since he had loved the king beyond words and had ministered to him the word of God. In all this relationship the young prince had responded with equal affection and appreciation.

There was poured out by all levels of society deep sorrow for the king's death with sincere weepings and lamentations comparable to those shown when King Josiah of Judah was struck by the fatal arrow of an Egyptian (2 Chron. 35:23-25). The life and works of King Edward reminded the people of England of that devout monarch of old, and they often spoke of their king as the "British Josiah," even centuries later.

There may still be at the top of the queen's staircase in Windsor Castle a statue of King Edward VI, marking with his sceptre, which he holds in his left hand, a passage in the Bible, and upon which he gazes intently. The passage is from 2 Chronicles 34:1, 2: *"Josiah was eight years old when he began to reign, and he reigned in Jerusalem one and thirty years. And he did that which was right in the sight of the Lord, and walked in the ways of David his father, and declined neither to the right hand, nor to the left."*

The most important feature of Edward's character was that he was a believer in the truth of the Bible, "a true saint of God," one of whom the world was not worthy.

John Calvin (1509-1564) a Reformer second only to *Martin Luther*, said in a letter to *Farell*, dated August 7, 1553, "Most truly do you say, that the land has been deprived of an incomparable treasure. Indeed I consider that, by the death of one youth

113

the whole nation has been bereaved of the best of fathers." [2]

The Legacy of the "British Josiah"

In cooperation with Ridley and the city administration, King Edward had provided generously for the poor.

At the commencement of Edward's last illness, Bishop Ridley preached before the king and said much about the duty of all believers to be charitable according to their ability, especially those of high rank. After the sermon the king sent for the bishop and asked him to sit down and be covered. He then went over the principal arguments mentioned in the sermon, desiring Ridley, that as he had shown what was the king's duty, would he now show him in what manner the king should perform it.

Bishop Ridley was deeply affected, even to tears, at this pleasing conduct of the king, and asked leave to consult with the mayor and the aldermen of London upon the subject. Edward approved of this, and desired that they would consider the best manner of relieving the poor.

Having taken the advice of the Lord Mayor and the aldermen of London, Ridley shortly returned to the king and stated that there were three classes of poor people.

[2] G. C. Gorham, *Gleanings of a Few Scattered Ears, During the Period of the Reformation in England*, Bell and Daldy, London.

First, there were the poor by impotency of nature, as young fatherless children, old decrepit persons, idiots, cripples and such like. These required education and maintenance. For them accordingly the king gave up Grey Friar's Monastery with the lands belonging to it, to be endowed as a school [now called Christ's Hospital].

Others, it was observed, were poor by faculty, as wounded soldiers, diseased and sick persons who required to be cured and relieved. For their use the king gave St. Bartholomew's near Smithfield.

The third sort were poor by idleness or unthriftiness, as vagabonds, loiterers who should be chastised and reduced to good order. For these the king appointed his house at Bridewell, the ancient mansion of many English kings.

He also provided for the relief of poor housekeepers.

The king hastened the appropriation of these endowments to the worthy purposes just described. He signed the charters on June 26, 1553, when he was so weak as scarcely able to hold the pen. He thanked God for sparing his life until he had executed this design.

Do we find in English history any other royal benefactor like him? The eyes of this king had been opened of God to know and to receive eternal life, and this constrained the dear, young monarch to make these generous endowments for the needy.

He founded no less than sixteen grammar schools and had plans to erect twelve colleges for the education of the young people.

Sir John Cheke, writing to Henry Bullinger less than a month before the king died, with heart-felt passion concerning the young prince he had helped to instruct in the things of God, said, "I prophesy indeed, that with the Lord's blessing, he will prove such a king, as neither to yield to Josiah in the maintenance of true religion, nor to Solomon in the management of the state, nor to David in the encouragement of godliness. He has removed images from the churches; he has overthrown idolatry; he has abolished the mass and destroyed almost every kind of superstition. He has put forth by his authority an excellent form of Common Prayer and he has published homilies to lessen ignorance of uneducated ministers." [3]

In the six short years of his reign the nation had been revolutionized. The foundations for the enlargement of true Christianity in England were laid in the encouragement given to the people to read, mark, learn and inwardly digest the word of God; and Rome, found this an insurmountable barrier to her incessant warfare for the subjugation of England century after century.

[3] *Writings of Edward the Sixth*, 1831.

The extended circulation of the Bible must ever be considered as one of the principal glories of King Edward's reign. The struggles of Wicliffe and Tyndale were rewarded. The freedom in the use of the Scriptures now was permitted to all when formerly reading the English Bible had been a serious criminal offense. No less than thirty-four editions of the whole Bible, or of the New Testament were printed during the six years Edward VI was upon the throne of England, beside partial portions of the Scriptures and innumerable other writings setting forth truths of the gospel of the living Savior.

The doctrinal articles which he was instrumental in preparing along with Cranmer were the basis for the *Thirty-Nine Articles* of the Church of England developed in the reign of Queen Elizabeth several years hence. Admittedly during that period the principle of full toleration in matters of religion was not understood or recognized even by the Protestants. However an important step towards religious liberty had been made. Although a declaration of assent to these articles was required of all who were public teachers in the church, the royal command to this effect did not direct any compulsory measures to enforce subscription, or any severe proceedings, unless the articles were openly withstood or denied. In that case the Council was to be informed, that such action might be taken as appeared requisite.

The serious reader cannot peruse the selection

of the prayers of the Edward VI *Primer* included in the compass of this book, without real spiritual profit. These may be considered as productions of the youthful monarch, though not immediately from his pen. His profound message in the *Treatise Against the Primacy of the Pope*, which is part of this volume, is most instructive, and will never cease to amaze the reader—that a prince, scarcely twelve years of age, was enabled to write it. The Spirit of God Himself was the king's illuminator.

A sufficient memorial of King Edward VI will never be wanting so long as a TRUE Christian faith is proclaimed and believed in England because *God* opened the eyes of one English king.

⤜ 12 ⤛

The Sad Interlude

Edward died on July 6, 1553; on July 9, Lady Jane Grey—who fainted when the idea was first broached to her—was proclaimed queen by Northumberland and his henchmen. Mary Tudor, having the support of many noblemen and the common people, gathered thousands of troops and marched on London, where on July 19th the mayor and aldermen proclaimed Mary Queen of England.

The duke of Northumberland was the first to experience her savage treatment. He was condemned and brought to the scaffold to die and suffer as traitor. Because of his sordid and inordinate ambitions, he died unpitied and unlamented.

The next victim was the amiable *Lady Jane Grey,* who had been compelled to accept the crown and thereby incurred Mary's displeasure.

However it must be noted that Queen Mary seemed eager to spare the life of Lady Jane Grey. Her execution was delayed until February 9, 1554, when *Renard* the zealous papal legate and the Emperor, Charles V, insisted that Lady Jane Grey was a threat and should be removed. The Emperor wrote, "Let the Queen's mercy be tempered with a little severity."

Jane was told that if she embraced the Roman Catholic faith, her life would be spared. This, however the staunch young Christian girl would not do. Before her execution she wrote to her sister Katherine and exhorted her, "Live still to die, deny the world, deny the Devil and despise the flesh. Take up your cross. As touching my death, rejoice, as I do, and adsist that I shall be delivered from corruption and put on incorruption. Farewell, dear sister, put your only trust in God, Who only must uphold you. Your loving sister, Jane Dudley." [1]

"When she first mounted the scaffold, she spoke earnestly to the spectators, 'Good people, touching the procurement of the crown on my behalf, I do wash my hands thereof in innocency before God. I did not desire it . . . I pray, good Christian people, to bear me witness, that I die a good Christian woman, and that I do look to be saved by no other means, but by the mercy of God in the blood of His only Son Jesus Christ: and I confess when I did know the word of God, I neglected the same, loved myself and the world, and thereby this plague and punishment is worthily happened unto me, and

[1] Alison Weir, *The Children of Henry VIII*, Ballantine Books, New York, 1996.

120

yet I thank God that of His goodness He hath thus given me time to repent.' She kneeled down and asked permission to say a Psalm. Then she said the Psalm of *Miserere mei Deus,* in English, in a most devout manner: Here is the Psalm—57:

> *Be merciful unto me, O God, be merciful unto me:*
> *For my soul trusteth in Thee: yea in the shadow of*
> *Thy wings will I make my refuge,*
> *Until these calamities be overpast.*
>
> *I will cry unto God most high:*
> *Unto God that performeth all things for me.*
>
> *He shall send from heaven, and save*
> *From the reproach of him*
> *That would swallow me up. Selah.*
> *God shall send forth His mercy and His truth.*
>
> *My soul is among lions:*
> *And I lie even among them*
> *That are set on fire, even the sons of men,*
> *Whose teeth are spears and arrows,*
> *And their tongue a sharp sword.*
>
> *Be Thou exalted, O God, above the heavens;*
> *Let Thy glory be above all the earth.*
>
> *They have prepared a net for my steps;*
> *My soul is bowed down:*
> *They have digged a pit before me,*
> *Into the midst whereof*
> *They are fallen themselves. Selah.*
>
> *My heart is fixed, O God,*
> *My heart is fixed:*
> *I will sing and give praise.*
> *Awake up, my glory; awake, psaltery and harp:*
> *I myself will awake early.*
>
> *I will praise Thee, O Lord, among the people:*
> *I will sing unto Thee among the nations.*
>
> *For Thy mercy is great unto the heavens,*
> *And Thy truth unto the clouds.*

Be Thou exalted, O God, above the heavens:
Let Thy glory be above all the earth.

Then she laid her head on the block, and said, 'Lord into Thy hands I commend my spirit.' Thus the dear sixteen-year-old saint of God completed her earthly sojourn on February 12, 1554."[2]

"The tragedy of Mary's reign," we are told in the Encyclopedia Brittanica, "was the belief not only that the Roman Catholic Church of her mother's day should be restored, but also that it could be best served by fire and blood."[3] She was utterly destitute of the truth of God's word and on fire with zeal for the traditions of Rome.

During her brief reign 288 persons were burned at the stake because they were Protestants—they believed the word of God. They were not rebels against the Queen's authority. They were not thieves or robbers, or murderers, or drunkards, or such as lived immoral lives. On the contrary, they were, almost without exception, among the purest, holiest and best Christians in England, and several of them the most learned men of their day.

The Burning of William Hunter

"It was the spring of the year 1555, when *William Hunter,* seventeen, entered the church to

[2] William Byron Forbush, editor, *Foxe's book of Martyrs*, John C. Winston Co., Philadelphia, 1926.

[3] *Encyclopedia Britannica,* Vol. 3, The University of Chicago, Chicago, 1974.

read the Book he loved. As he stood reading the word of God, *Atwell,* an officer of the popish bishop saw him. 'Why meddlest thou with the Bible. Knowest thou how to read? And canst thou expound the Scriptures?' William replied modestly, 'I take not upon me to expound the Scriptures; but finding the Bible here, I read it to my comfort.'

"The officer began to speak scornfully of the Sacred Word. 'Say not so,' William said respectfully, 'it is God's book, out of which every one that hath grace may learn to know what pleaseth God, and what is displeasing to Him.'

"When Atwell could not prevail with the lad, he cried, 'I see you are one who dislikes the Queen's laws, but if you do not turn, you as well as many other heretics, will broil for your opinions.'

" 'God give me grace,' William replied meekly, 'that I may believe His word, and confess His name, whatever may come of it.'

" 'Confess His name!' shouted Atwell, 'No, no; you will go to the devil, all of you.'

"Atwell left quickly and came back with a priest. William knew what lay ahead, he hastened to his father's house, related what happened, and fled from the town.

"A few days later a justice ordered his father to produce his son. On learning the danger of his parent, William went home. It was with heavy hearts and weeping that the father and son greeted each other. During the night William was seized, and hurried to the stocks. Early in the morning, the justice of the peace tried to shake his faith, and then carried him to the old palace in the fields of Bethnal Green—about 16 miles away—where *Bonner*, the popish bishop resided. The evil bishop first spoke to him gently, then sternly, and then roughly, but still William would not promise to give up the Bible and deny the truth.

"The bishop sent William to one of the London prisons, with strict orders to the jailer to put as many iron chains upon him as he could possibly bear. He was confined in that dungeon for nine months, trusting God and praying.

"The wicked Bonner sent for him, but the spirit of the young martyr remained unbroken. 'If you recant,' said the bishop, 'I will give you forty pounds, set you up in business and make you steward of my own house.' 'But my lord,' was William's reply, 'if you cannot persuade my conscience by Scripture, I cannot find it in my heart to turn from God for the love of the world.'

"When neither threats nor promises availed, the only thing that remained for him was the fire. At length the morning came when dear William was to die. As he was led along, his father rushed forwards and in agony of parental feeling, throwing his arms around the neck of his noble son, he said, with tears flowing, 'God be with thee, son, William.' There were *many* weeping eyes on that sad day in the little town of Brentwood. He bade farewell to those who had been his playmates and friends of earlier days.

"Without loss of time he was secured by a chain, and wood was piled around. Another pardon was offered him if he would profess himself a papist. 'No.' said William resolutely, 'I will not recant, God willing.' Then turning to the people he asked them to pray for him.

" 'Pray for thee?' cried a wicked justice who was looking on, 'I will no more pray for thee than I would pray for a dog.' A priest, too, began to taunt him; until a Christian gentleman spoke aloud, 'May God have mercy on his soul,' and the people mournfully added a loud 'Amen.'

"The fire was now lighted, and as the flames began to rise, William, who still held in his hand a book of Psalms, threw it into the hands of his brother, who had followed him to the place of death. 'William,' his brother called, 'think of the sufferings of Christ and be not afraid.'

" 'I am not afraid,' added the martyr. 'Lord, Lord, receive my spirit.' Those were his last words.

"An old elm tree still marks the spot near which William was burned for the sake of the truth."[4]

[4] *Historical Tales for Young Protestants*, Wycliffe Press, London.

The Burning of
Hugh Latimer and Nicholas Ridley

Then Queen Mary turned on the leading English Reformers.

Hugh Latimer (1485-1555) was the first for whom a warrant was issued. For six fruitful years, living under the hospitable roof of Lambeth Palace belonging to Cranmer, he took an active part in all the measures adopted for carrying forward the Protestant Reformation in England. In the first years of Edward's reign he preached before the King's court at regular weekly intervals. More than any other man in England he promoted the Reformation by his preaching.

Now, in 1554, Latimer was committed to the Tower of London, in company with Cranmer, Ridley and Bradford. For want of room, all four were confined to one chamber.

From the Tower the three Bishops were removed to Oxford; and there in 1555 Latimer and Nicholas Ridley, bishop of London, were burnt alive at the stake. Latimer said, "I read the New Testament over seven times while I was in prison." Much of his time was spent in prayer. *Augustine Bernher,* his faithful servant, tells us that Latimer, by now aged and infirm, continued kneeling in prayer so long that often he was not able to get up from his knees without help. Three things he pleaded daily: One, that as God had appointed him to be a preacher of His Word, so He would give him His grace to stand up for this doctrine in the fire. Second, that God in His great mercy would restore the Gospel to the realm of England once again. The third was, that God would preserve the Princess Elizabeth and make her a comfort to England.

In a remarkable way all three of these prayers were fully granted.

"The place appointed for the execution," says *Foxe,* "was on the north side of Oxford, in the ditch over against Balliol College." The Queen, for fear of a tumult, had commanded the city officials to be sufficiently armed.

Latimer and Ridley, with an iron chain about their middles, were fastened to the stake. A bag of gunpowder was tied about the neck of each. Faggots were piled around them, and now the horrible preparations were completed.

"Then they brought a faggot kindled with fire," Foxe tells us, "and laid it down at Ridley's feet, to whom Latimer then spake in this manner: BE OF GOOD COMFORT, BROTHER RIDLEY, AND PLAY THE MAN; WE SHALL THIS DAY LIGHT SUCH A CANDLE, BY GOD'S GRACE IN ENGLAND, AS I TRUST NEVER SHALL BE PUT OUT."

The fire being kindled, Ridley cried with a loud voice, "Lord, into Thy hands I commend my spirit:

Lord receive my spirit." Latimer prayed similarly, "Father of heaven, receive my soul!"

The two giants of the faith soon died amidst the flames of their bigoted Queen.

Could it not be said that the "candle" which they hoped to light in England was already lit, and their heroic martyrdom was adding fuel to that candle which was lighted while the young king, whose eyes God had opened, was on the throne of England.

The burning of Cranmer came soon after.

"Mary's reign was a study in failure. Her husband, who was ten years her junior, remained in England as little as possible; the war between France and the Hapsburg Empire into which her Spanish marriage had dragged the kingdom, was a disaster and resulted in the loss of England's last continental outpost, Calais": the jewel city in France. [5] Her people quite generally learned to call her "Bloody Mary," (an appellation which might more suitably be attributed to the bad, blind and bloody popes, whose barbaric orders Mary zealously pursued) and greeted the news of her death on November 17, 1558, without lamentation.

On November 17, 1558, Mary's sister, Elizabeth (daughter of Henry VIII and *Anne Boleyn*) became Queen of England with great jubilation on the part of the people, with ringing of bells and bonfires.

[5] *Encyclopedia Britannica,* Vol. 3, The University of Chicago, Chicago, 1974.

⁓ *13* ⁓

Epilogue: The Flowering of the English Reformation

Elizabeth, daughter of Henry VIII and Anne Boleyn, became queen of England when Queen Mary died on November 17, 1558. She was a Protestant but she moved cautiously. Her religious settlement of 1559 enforced the Protestant faith by law, but was not unduly harsh to the Roman Catholics until the interdict of *Pope Pius V* against Elizabeth. Thereafter the treatment of English Catholics became increasingly severe; the disobedient were imprisoned or they paid fines, but the disobedient Catholics were not burned as the Protestants were in the reign of Queen Mary.

There was a custom in England that on the coronation of a monarch certain prisoners would be released. When this had been done following the coronation of Elizabeth, certain lords came to Elizabeth and said, "There are four or five others to be freed."

"Ah, who are they?" she asked.

"Matthew, Mark, Luke, John and Paul" was the answer, "they have been long shut up so that they could not talk to the common people, who are eager to send them abroad again." Elizabeth was glad enough to let the evangelists go free and the preaching of the gospel of Christ resumed throughout the land. A law was passed to the effect that "every parish church should be provided with a Bible, and that every parson should have a New Testament for his own private use." Before the close of the reign of Elizabeth there were two hundred and sixteen editions of the Bible issued from the English press, a great many more than were published in all the other parts of Europe.

The Protestant Reformation in England was wonderfully blessed of God and people all over the nation, young and old, saw the light of the Gospel and a new way of life was begun.

What is the Gospel?

The central thrust of the Protestant Reformation in England was the preaching of the Gospel. For centuries they had been living in darkness and ignorance. Some of it sounds incredible. The religious practice of Roman Catholicism had degenerated into a shoddy variety of simony as the narrative that follows illustrates.

Here is a group moving about under the banner,

"The Salvation of the Soul." These dealers pass through the country in a gay carriage with three horsemen by their side. As they came near to a town, the magistrates, priests, nuns and the trades went forth to welcome them with music, tapers and ringing of bells. Three monks seat themselves at a table and raise a red flag, having on it the Pope's coat-of-arms. Before them is a money-chest: and now one of them named *Tetzel* (1465-1519) begins the sale. "Come near," he cried aloud, "and I will give you indulgences—letters duly sealed, by which even the sins you hereafter commit shall be all forgiven you: even repentance is not necessary. But more than this; these letters will not only save the living, but also the dead. The very moment the money clinks against the bottom of the chest, the soul escapes from purgatory (the place of punishment where the souls are supposed to be cleansed by fire) and flies to heaven. Bring your money; bring money; bring money." [1]

The whole account of this shameful imposture is almost too shocking for the mind to accept.

But what is the Gospel of Jesus Christ according to the Scripture that was recovered in the Protestant Reformation in England?

A person is saved by faith alone in Jesus Christ alone! Such faith always involves repentance.

---

[1] *Historical Tales for Young Protestants,* Wycliffe Press, London.

From Scripture we have it in a nutshell stated in John 3:16, "For God so loved the world that He gave His only begotten Son that whosoever believeth in Him should not perish but have everlasting life."

And in Acts 4:12, we read, "Neither is there salvation in any other: for there is none other name under heaven given among men, whereby we must be saved.":

> "For this did many a martyr bleed,
> The noble and the brave,
> That truth its onward course might speed,
> Men of all lands and tongues be freed,
> And life eternal have."

Martin Luther, (1483-1546) in Germany, shook the continent when he boldly and fearlessly declared, *"The just shall live by faith"* (Hab. 2:4; Rom. 1:17).

Paul gave us the essence of the whole Gospel in a couple of verses: "But now the righteousness of God without law is manifested, being witnessed by the law and the prophets; even the righteousness of God which is by faith of Jesus Christ unto all and upon all them that believe" (Rom. 3:21, 22). Faith in Jesus Christ is the one and only complete condition for salvation.

Faith is but a simple confidence in God. There is no more value or merit in faith than there is in a man's works, but it is the God-constituted medium through which a person receives the gift of righteousness. It is not faith, itself, but the object of that faith—the Lord Jesus Christ—who saves the person. Faith is but the feeble, trembling hand that touches the mighty Savior.

Faith is but a simple act in which one person, a sinner, commits himself to another Person, the Savior. Faith is as immediate as a lightening thunderbolt. It strikes and the eternal transaction is completed. At that moment, God makes an effectual grant of perfect righteousness—even the righteousness of Christ—"upon all them that believe." In this gracious act, God absolves them forever from the guilt and punishment of sin, and bestows upon them His own everlasting righteousness which is infinitely superior to what Adam had before the fall.

Think upon it, believer, and rejoice! It is not a righteousness that is earned before or after salvation, but one that is freely donated and put upon the one who does nothing more—yet nothing less—than believe upon Christ, the Son of the living God. The prophet Isaiah exulted in the reality of this glorious truth: "He has clothed me with the robe of righteousness . . . My salvation shall be forever, and my righteousness shall not be abolished" (6:10; 51:6).

Thomas Chalmers (1780-1847), perhaps the greatest preacher of Scotland, had a remarkable conversion some years after he had begun preaching and he was very exacting on the subject of salvation. "The foundation of your trust before God," he said, "must either be your own righteousness out and out, or the righteousness of Christ, out and out . . . . If you are to lean upon your own merit, lean upon it wholly—if you are to lean upon Christ, lean upon Him wholly. The two will not amalgamate together; and it is the attempt to make them do so, which keeps many a weary and heavy-laden inquirer at a distance from rest, and at a distance from the truth of the gospel. Maintain a clear and consistent posture. Stand not before God with one foot upon a rock and the other upon treacherous quicksand . . . We call you to lean not so much as the weight of one grain or scruple of your confidence upon your own doings—to leave this ground entirely, and to come over entirely to the ground of a Redeemer's blood and a Redeemer's righteousness." [2]

Even the most devout Roman Catholics, in all generations, never have had an assurance of salvation if they follow their own Catholic doctrines. *Dr. Harry A. Ironside* (1876-1951), for many years pastor of the Moody Memorial Church in Chicago, worked closely with some Roman Catholics. He said that he asked them, "Suppose the pope dies, does he go to heaven?

"Oh, no," they reply, "They are having masses still for Pope Leo XIII (1810-1903), who was a great scholar and a great churchman."

Then Dr. Ironside goes on to tell about the

[2] Thomas Chalmers, *Sermons and Discourses,* Robert Carter & Brothers, New York, 1881.

complete lack of assurance about salvation. "When a child comes into the world, the Church of Rome baptises him as soon as possible, and if you say, 'Why is the child baptized?' the answer is, 'To cleanse him from original sin and make him a member of Christ.' But when he grows up, you ask, 'Is the child cleansed from original sin, is he a member of Christ?' and they answer, *'We do not know.'*

"The boy grows and becomes conscious of sin, he goes to confession and the priest lays certain penances upon him. Through the sacrament of penance, through his own contrition, added to the infinite merit of our Lord Jesus Christ, he is supposed to find forgiveness. When his penance has been completed, you say, 'Now is your soul saved?' And the answer will be, *'I do not know.'* He goes through life making confession after confession, and doing penance again and again, and at last he is dying. He lies on his deathbed, the priest is summoned and gives him the holy communion for the last time, and the sacrament of extreme unction, and anoints him for his death. He passes away, and as he lies there with the crucifix on his breast, you look down upon him and say to his friends, 'Is he saved now? Is he with Christ?' They say, *'We do not know.'* Masses are often said and paid for, sometimes for years, and at the end of scores of such services, you go to the priest and say, 'Well, is our friend out of purgatory now, is he with Christ in heaven?' and he replies, *'We do not know.' "*

This lack of any assurance of salvation is due to a lack of believing what the Bible tells us.

The Means of the Reformation in England

The Reformation in England was essentially accomplished by the holy Scriptures. There were no outstanding personages in England like we meet in Germany, in Switzerland, in France—Luther, Zwingli and Calvin. "The Lord sends his hearers to the Scriptures and not to the church" was a simple principle laid down by Cranmer. "But," replied the monks, "they are so difficult." "Explain obscure passages by those that are clear," rejoined Cranmer, "Scripture by Scripture. Seek, pray, and he who has the key of David will open them to you." [3]

Erasmus (1466-1536), who died the same year as did Tyndale, earnestly called for a translation of the Bible into the vulgar tongue, "so that the husbandman should sing them as he holds the handle of the plough, the weaver repeat them as he plies his shuttle, and the wearied traveller, halting on his journey, refresh himself under some shady tree by these godly narratives." Erasmus ventured out on the laborious task of collating the Greek manuscripts of the New Testament then available to him. He had the Greek text printed in Basel, Switzerland, and the

[3] J. H. Merle d'Aubigne, *The Reformation in England,* Vol. 1, Banner of Truth Trust, London, 1962.

pure Word of God was thus available for translation by Coverdale, Tyndale and others. [4]

Then in the good providence of God there came a young king "Josiah" who embraced the word of God in his own heart and had it proclaimed to the people of his realm. This was interrupted for a few years by Queen Mary, the unfortunate slave of popery, and then the truth of the Gospel blossomed throughout the land under the reign of Queen Elizabeth. The Reformation by the word of God brought about a spiritual Christianity which the power of hierarchal Romanism had previously destroyed in the course of centuries all over Europe.

Following Elizabeth, *James VI* of Scotland became king of England as *James I.* Shortly after the festivities of the coronation were over, a great council was held in the winter of 1604, at Hampton Court Palace, a few miles from London. The chief purpose of this meeting was to consider a new translation of the Bible. This great work was done by fifty-four of the most learned and distinguished Bible scholars in England. One of that group whose spiritual stature stands high to this day was *Lancelot Andrewes.* In 1611 it was published as the "King James" or "Authorized Version" of the holy Scriptures. That version retained its ascendancy for more than three hundred and fifty years, and to this day many in the English speaking world regard it as the

[4] Ibid.

most acceptable translation, though, of course, no translation is perfect.

> "We'll prize our English Bible then—
> What suffering it has cost!
> What tears and groans of godly men,
> Who won it with their mortal pain,
> That we might not be lost."

The Blessings of the Reformation

The word of God, believed and cherished, brings maturity, wisdom and strength to the believer in every generation.

In the wake of the great Bible Reformation in England, there were spiritual giants in the land and a wave of productivity in the various areas of learning flourished—including literary, musical, scientific and other spheres of knowledge.

We speak first of the oft-ridiculed Puritans, "the most remarkable body of men, perhaps, which the world has ever produced," as *Lord Macaulay* (1800-1859) labels them. Their dress, their manners, their Hebrew names are but surface things which amuse the worldlings and provide grist for the shallow philosophers. The Puritans were people whose minds had derived a deep spiritual character as a result of daily contemplation of the Scriptures and eternal interests. They desired no higher recognition than the favor of God. For them death had lost its terrors and the world its charms. "They went through the world," Macaulay continues, "like

Sir Artegal's iron man Talus with his flail, crushing and trampling down oppressors, mingling with human beings, but having neither part nor lot in human infirmities, insensible to fatigue, to pleasure and to pain, not to be pierced by any weapon, not to be withstood by any barrier." [5]

The pervasive influence of the Puritans crossed the Atlantic and showed itself in the character of the hardy settlers who began to lay the foundations for the United States of America.

One hesitates even to mention the long list of statesmen, preachers, musicians, and scientists who distinguished themselves in their liberated England and whose works continue to bless the hearts of God's people throughout the world. We speak of *Shakespeare,* the greatest of all writers, with his tragedies and comedies teeming with wisdom and allusions to the Bible. We speak of the blind poet *John Milton* and his immortal "Paradise Lost." We speak of *Edmund Spenser* and his "Faerie Queene," a powerful allegory on the Christian virtues.

Isaac Watts had the English people singing hymns whose lyrics had Bible substance and were expressed with poetic skill. *George Frideric Handel* turned the people, who had been listening to Italian operas whose language they did not understand, to compositions like his enduring *Messiah.* In the field

[5] Thomas Babington Macaulay, *Miscellaneous Essays and Poems,* T.Y. Crowell, New York.

of science *Isaac Newton,* head and shoulders above the rest, yet a humble believer in the Lord, reverenced and studied the holy Scriptures.

We now speak of *John Wesley* "whom the people heard gladly" and a spiritual revival sprang up all over Britain. He was assisted by his brother *Charles,* who excelled in music, and *George Whitfield,* who first introduced John Wesley to open-air preaching. These men exerted a far-reaching spiritual influence over the multitudes. This influence cannot be measured but it fostered the principles of the Reformation that began with Edward VI and it helped to keep England from falling into the cultural and spiritual morass which overtook some of the countries on the continent.

In Italy, the *Renaissance* gave rise to a new spirit of inquiry with men like *Galileo, Petrarch, Michaelangelo* and others. And although it was a return to classical values, it resulted mostly in the spread of humanism. There was no biblical revival and one reason was the fact that the whole country was held in the grip of Roman Catholicism and its pope.

In France, the whole country was devastated for ten chaotic years in what is known as the great *French Revolution* (1789-1799). The people followed the rebellious doctrines of *Rousseau* who seriously departed from Christian values and glorified natural goodness, including human nature. The net result was that of a diluted belief in a Supreme Being with whom there was no meaningful personal relationship on the part of those who accepted the philosophical tenets of that teaching.

In Great Britain, the people, liberated from the shackles of Roman Catholicism, were taught to reverence and accept the holy Scriptures. A spiritual revival followed in every area where those Scriptures were proclaimed. It was the Bible-based Christianity, begun in the sixteenth century that for many years kept the nation and its people from succumbing to the degrading philosophies that were spawned elsewhere.

And when we think of Britain's kings, the one who heads the list is King Edward VI, whose eyes God opened to understand the holy Scriptures and to trust the blessed Redeemer, the Lord Jesus Christ. In the short reign of this God-anointed king, the foundations of the Protestant Reformation were established and bountiful blessings of God followed.

> *"O Holy Spirit! who gave the word,*
> *With thine own truth Thy light afford,*
> *Give Thou the quickening, saving power,*
> *On all the earth Thy blessings shower."*

Preface

Treatise Against the Primacy of the Pope

The fact that a youth scarcely twelve years of age could write such a prodigious treatise as this seems incredible almost to the point of being unbelievable. Yet there is no reason to question Edward's authorship of the Treatise. It was quite obvious from his early years that not only was he generously endowed mentally but that he had a heart for the truth as it is revealed in the Bible and that he diligently pursued the study of it and found great delight in it.

Certainly Edward learned much from his teachers and from preachers like Cranmer, Ridley, Latimer and from the learned men on the continent, but when you read his exhaustive treatise you are compelled to believe that he simply had to study the Bible carefully for himself. And the fact that he wrote this amidst all the turmoil of the religious and political battles all around him causes us to believe that the Holy Spirit guided the young monarch in what he wrote. He began the composition December 13th 1548 and completed it on the last day of August 1549.

So far as we have been able to ascertain no one has raised any compelling objection about Edward's authorship of the treatise during his time or since then. Those who read it at the time it was written—like Henry Bullinger and John Calvin—fully attributed it to Edward and were highly impressed by it.

Real scholarship characterizes most of his writing, but then we come across those more difficult Bible passages where Edward struggles, repeats himself, and a full clarity of expression is lacking. There is enough of such to make us realize that the writer did not have many years of study and meditation in his mental storehouse. One has to conclude that the Holy Spirit motivated this dedicated young lad as he endeavored to express his pent up abhorrence of popery.

This superb treatise reveals the solidity of the young king's convictions and the depths of his Bible knowledge. Yet some of the biographers of Edward VI make no mention of this important work, and others give it only a passing recognition.

The reader will at once be impressed and even shocked at the strong and unequivocal words Edward uses, and then we have only to remember the times in which it was written. Actually Edward used some of the same words which the Roman Catholic hierarchy used to describe those who rejected the Roman Catholic teachings and authority. Tyndale in writing about the pope used some of the same strong words to describe him. The brutality of the popes during those centuries had no limits when dealing with people who questioned the papal doctrines and decrees. The actions of the popes and their legates were savage and devilish. In reading the chapter on the reign of "Bloody Mary" one can readily understand how Edward felt toward the pope whom Mary, his sister, obeyed so completely.

From our perspective, almost five hundred years later, more temperate language would be preferable, but we accept the young king's message in the context of the times.

Not much more than a century ago, *J. C. Ryle,* the distinguished Bible commentator and bishop of Liverpool in the Church of England, described the conditions then existing in words that would be hard to improve: "The night of the Middle ages was dark and wild. The three centuries immediately preceding the English Reformation in the middle of which Wicliffe lived, was probably the darkest period of history of English Christianity. It was a period when the Church of the land was thoroughly, entirely and completely Roman Catholic—when the Bishop of Rome was the spiritual head of the Church. Romanism reigned supreme and the people were all alike, papists. During these three centuries before the Reformation, England was buried under a mass of ignorance, superstition, priestcraft and immorality." [1]

At such a time came along this "tender heart," King Edward VI, born of the most unlikely parenthood, and quickly grew into a strong "voice in the wilderness," declaring the way of the Lord.

When *Calvin* and *Bullinger* first read this message they were deeply moved. Yet this treasure has remained buried in the archives of history for more than four centuries.

In the providence of God, it is now before us, and we have a responsibility as to how we let it speak to the people

[1] John Charles Ryle, *Light from Old Times,* Chas. J. Thynne, London, 1890.

144

of the world where much of the same ignorance and darkness prevails.

In preparing this book, the author felt impressed to let all the words of Edward VI stand as they were written by him. Here and there a clarifying word is included and this is indicated by the use of the brackets. The insertion of the subheadings is used to facilitate the reading of the treatise. We also supplied Scripture references with the Scriptures which Edward quoted.

Some clarity in the English version may have been lost in the translation from the French in which Edward wrote it, especially if the translator was unfamiliar with biblical terms and the theological vocabulary.

We are aware of the fact that Edward's message is not the kind that we normally come across, but we trust that God will use it to awaken believers—especially the leaders—of our generation to study and accept the truth of the Bible and weigh it and compare it with the false teachings that flourish in our day. May God use it to stir preachers and teachers to proclaim the true Gospel of Christ without fear and without compromise.

—*N. A. Woychuk*

Dedication

To my most dear and well-beloved Uncle, Edward, Duke of Somerset, Governor of my Person, and Protector of my Kingdoms, Countries, and Subjects.

After having considered, my dear and well-beloved uncle, how much they displease God, who waste all their time on the follies and vanities of this world . . . I have determined to employ myself about the doing something, which will be as I hope, profitable to myself, and acceptable unto you.

Having then considered, that we see many papists not only curse us, but call and name us heretics, because we have forsaken their Antichrist, and its traditions, and followed the light which God hath been pleased to afford us; we are inclined to write something to defend us against their contumelies, and lay them, as is just, upon their own backs.   For they call us heretics, but alas! they are so themselves, whilst

146

they forsake the pure voice of the gospel, and follow their own imaginations; as is most evident from Boniface the third, who thought, when he was made the universal bishop, that the falling away, which St. Paul speaks of in his second epistle to the Thessalonians, and second chapter, had happened in himself.

Considering then by your life and actions, that you have a great affection to the Divine word, and the sincere religion, I dedicate this present work to you, praying you to take it in good part. God give you His perpetual grace, and show His benignity upon you for ever.

From our Palace at Westminster, in London, this last day of August, 1549.

King Edward VI

Section 2

Treatise
Against the
Primacy of the Pope

by King Edward VI

We may easily find and perceive by the experience of
the world, that human nature is disposed to all evils, and
entangled by all manner of vices. For what nation is there
in the earth in which there is not some vice, and many
disorders? And principally in this age, because now there
is such an exaltation of the great empire of Antichrist;
which is the source of all evil, and the fountain of all
abomination, and true son of the devil.

For when God had sent His only Son to heal our
infirmities, and to reconcile the world unto Himself by
His death; the devil soon changed the institutions of
Christ into human traditions, and perverted the holy
Scriptures to his purposes and designs, by his minister
the pope. And therefore, if the astrologers, who maintain that all things shall return to their own elements,
say a truth, the pope shall descend into hell. For he
cannot belong unto God, or be His servant, whilst, under the pretence of religion, and the command of God,
he usurps unto himself the authority of Christ, as appears

148

in all his works. Therefore it seemed best to me, in this little book, first to condemn the papacy, and afterwards the doctrine of the pope. Though I am not ignorant that it is a difficult task, because there are many that will contradict it. Notwithstanding, we will condemn the supremacy of the pope from these following reasons.

Is Rome the Mother of All Churches?

Whereas the papists say, that Rome is the mother of all other churches, and therefore the bishop of Rome ought to be superior to all other bishops, I answer that it is impossible; because the first promise was made unto the Jews: now Rome was then heathen, and Jerusalem was Christian; for St. Paul, writing to the Romans, says, "Through their fall, salvation is come unto the Gentiles" (Rom. 11:11).

And because the papists cannot prove Rome to have been the mother of all the other churches, they therefore say the bishop of Rome hath received his power from St. Peter to whom had been given the same authority with Christ, and remains in the said bishop of Rome to this day. They endeavor to prove this out of the following texts, "Thou art Peter, and upon this rock I will build my church," saith Christ (Matt. 16:18); and a little after, "And I will give thee the keys of the kingdom of heaven," (Matt. 16:19). They allege from another holy Scripture, where Peter says to Christ, "Lord, Thou knowest that I love Thee," (Jn. 21:15), meaning, that he that loves Christ is the chiefest, and Peter loving Christ more than any of the other apostles loved Him, is thereby the chief and principal of the apostles.

Again, they affirm that he only was commanded to "feed the sheep" of Christ (Jn. 21:16), and to be the fisher of men; and that he was the first speaker, and made answer to Jesus, "Behold here are two swords" (Lu. 22:38); from whence the papists conclude, that Peter had a temporal and a spiritual sword.

They allege also some human reasons, that as the bees have one king, so all Christians ought to have one pope. And that as there was of old amongst the Jews, a principal priest or bishop, as Moses and Aaron, so now it is necessary there should be a bishop of bishops.

Here are two great falsehoods in these few words: the one is, that the authority and supremacy over the church was given to St. Peter: the other, that Peter was at Rome.

The Church Was Not Founded Upon Peter

To the first, where they say that that authority was given him by these words, "Thou art Peter," etc. I answer, that if you remark [notice] the preceding and following words in that chapter of the gospel, you will find that Christ did not speak of Peter, as he was barely a man, but as [because] he was a believer. For the foregoing words are, how Peter had said, "Thou art the Son of God": by which it is evident, that Christ did not say, that Peter was the foundation of the church, but [that He] spoke of the *faith* of Peter.

In Matthew 16:23, Christ called Peter, "Satan"; but the church of God is not founded upon Satan, therefore it is not founded upon Peter. For if the church was founded upon St. Peter, it would have a weak foundation: and like

150

that house which was built on a sandy foundation, which could not stand long, but the floods came, and the winds blew, and beat upon that house and it fell (Matt. 7:26). In like manner the church would fall, if it had so poor a foundation. By which one may see that these words in the text, "Thou art Peter, and upon this rock will I build my church," must not be understood of Peter, but of the faith of Peter, upon which the church is founded. But he was a frail and weak vessel, and denied Christ thrice.

The Keys Were Given to All the Apostles

Their second text is, that the keys of heaven were given to St. Peter. To which I answer, that the keys were given not only to Peter, but also to the other apostles. And by this argument I answer, that he was not principal; because the rest received the same authority of the keys, that was committed to him.

On which account, St. Paul calls St. Peter the pillar, not the foundation of the church; his companion, not his governor (Gal. 2:5-9). And what arc the keys of heaven? The authority of pardoning sins? No, it is the preaching of the gospel of God the Father, the gospel, I say, of God; not the pope's or devil's. And as when a door is open, every one who will, may enter therein; so when God sent His gospel, He opened truth, which is the gate of heaven: and gave unto men an understanding of the scriptures, which if they obeyed [believed], they should thereby be saved (2 Cor. 2:3-6) [probably means 2 Corinthians 2]. By which we see that the gospel and the truth of the scriptures are the only gates that conduct men to the kingdom of God.

A Believer's Faith is Counted for Righteousness

Whence St. Paul says in Rom. 10:13-17: "Whosoever shall call upon the name of the Lord, shall be saved: how then shall they call on Him in whom they have not believed? And how shall they believe in Him of whom they have not heard? And how shall they hear without a preacher? And a little after, he saith, "So then faith cometh by hearing, and hearing by the word of God." And in the fourth chapter to the Romans, he also saith, "But to him that worketh not, but believeth on Him that justifieth the ungodly, his faith is counted for righteousness" (4:5). Moreover, we will prove that the preaching of the gospel is the key of heaven: in the tenth chapter to the Romans Paul affirms that, "Whoever calls upon the name of the Lord, shall be saved"; and that the preaching of the gospel is the door that leads to the invocation of the name of God; whence it follows, that the preaching of the gospel is the way and entrance of salvation.

Faith is the Basis for Justification

Again, Paul affirms that faith justifies, and that the preaching of the gospel causes [brings] faith, which I have showed before, whence it follows that the true preaching of the word is the door and entrance to justification. Like as ground which is sowed may [will] produce fruit, if the seed be not cast into ground which is full of thistles, or thorns, or stones; and yet although it be sowed in such ground, it will a little meliorate [improve] the earth. So, if the word of God be sowed in the hearts of honest people, or such as have a zeal for truth, it will confirm them in all goodness; but if any be obstinate and perverse, they cannot impute [attribute] the fault unto the holy Scriptures, which is really in themselves.

Therefore we ought to do our utmost endeavours to cause the gospel to be preached throughout all the world; as it is written, "All power is given unto Me in heaven and in earth: go ye therefore, and teach all nations, baptizing them in My name" (Matt. 28:18; Mark 16:15, 16; Lu. 24:47, 48).

Peter Compared with Paul

Since then it is proved that the keys of heaven is the authority of preaching; and that the authority of preaching was given to *all* the apostles, I cannot see how, by that text, any more authority was given to Peter than to the other disciples: and St. Paul says, he himself was not a "whit behind the very chiefest apostles" (2 Cor. 11:5).

Then, if he [what Paul] said [is] true, St. Peter was not above him: and if I were asked which of them was the better, I should say Paul, because he preached more than they all.

But we ought to account certainly, that the Spirit of God was poured out upon them all; and that the same Spirit of God which filled St. Peter, filled also St. Paul: from whence may be proved that neither of them was superior to the other.

Again, the papists say, that after Christ was raised from the dead, He asked who loved Him, and that Peter answered, he loved Him, and therefore, say they, he was the chief apostle.

By which reason, every good man ought to have the supremacy over every other, because each good and pious person loves God; for it is the duty and office of every true Christian. Now the question is not, whether Peter was faithful, pious, good, a holy and true Christian, but whether he was principal, head, governor, and king above and over the rest of the apostles and ministers of Jesus Christ? For, if the pope would have the authority of St. Peter, which was to preach, I would be content to give it to him. But he regards but little the precept of God; for Jesus departed into a mountain alone, when He perceived the Jews would make him a king and emperor: and the pope by wrong, or violence, or deceit, hath made all nations subject unto himself.

Contrast between Jesus and Pope

Jesus wore a crown of thorns, and a purple robe was thrown upon Him in derision, and all the multitude mocked and spat upon Him—but the pope decks himself with a triple crown, and is adored by kings, princes, emperors, and all estates of persons. Jesus washed His disciples' feet—and kings kiss the feet of the pope. Jesus paid tribute—but the pope receives tribute, and pays none. Jesus opened His mouth and taught the people—the pope takes his ease and rest in his castle of St. Angelo. Jesus healed all diseases—the pope rejoices in blood and massacres. Christ bore His cross upon his shoulders—the pope is borne upon the shoulders of men.

Christ came with peace and poverty into the world— the pope delights in stirring up war amongst the kings and princes of the earth. Christ came meekly, humbly, and compassionately, sitting upon an ass—but the pope rides in all pomp and splendor. Christ was a lamb—the pope is a wolf. Christ was poor—the pope would have all Christian kingdoms under his power and command. Christ drove the money-changers and sellers out of the temple—the pope brings them in.

Jesus instituted the sacrament in simple commemoration of Himself—the pope formed the mass, a masterpiece of imposture. Jesus ascended into heaven—and the pope falls into hell. God hath commanded that we should have no other God but Him—and the pope makes himself to be honored like unto a great God. God forbids us to commit idolatry—and the pope is the author of image-worship. God hath prohibited swearing in vain—but the pope allows his friends perjury. God hath commanded the use of festivals in good works, prayers and devotions—but the pope allows pomp, games, idleness, and mimicry to be exercised on those days in churches. God hath forbidden murder—and killing any person—and it is a matter of great compassion and sorrow, to see how cruelly the pope persecuted Christians. God foretold this persecution in Matthew 24:11-16. "Many false prophets," said Christ, "shall arise at that time; and because iniquity shall abound, the love of many shall wax cold; but the gospel shall be preached in all the world; when ye therefore shall see the abomination of desolation, spoken of by Daniel the prophet, stand in the holy place, then let them which be in Judea, flee into the mountains." And is not this come to pass now? Yea, for there are many wolves in sheep's clothing; who under the pretence of religion, obscure the true doctrine of Christ; and almost all abominations were introduced into the holy place, that is to say, brought into the church of God.

But to return to our matter, God forbids adultery—notwithstanding, the pope, who will be obedient to his father the devil, commands his priests to keep several concubines and harlots, rather than join themselves to any in marriage. God hath forbid stealing from either man, woman or child—but the pope is such an old thief, that he robs even God of His honor, and transfers it to himself. God hath forbid bearing false witness against anyone—but the pope cries that all is good grist which comes to his mill. God hath commanded us to be content with what is our own—but the pope will have every house pay him a tribute; to conclude, he is in every thing opposite to God.

But I cannot blame him, for he fulfills the command of Paul, which says, "Children, obey your parents," and the demon of hypocrisy is his father, to whom he pays all obedience. "The devil walketh about as a roaring lion," saith St. Peter, "seeking whom he may devour." And does not the pope do the same? Yea certainly, for he not only ordains wicked and unjust laws; but he pursues to death, all who have a true zeal and love towards God.

Look at the Primacy of Peter Again

But to return to the primacy of Peter. I ask, how many kingdoms St. Peter had under his dominion? For it was impossible that all kingdoms should be under him, when St. James was then bishop of Jerusalem, and that city was not then Christian. Neither can I see how Peter should be the chief: for St. Paul says to the Corinthians concerning the apostles, "All are yours, and you are Christ's, and Christ is God's." Likewise, St. Peter calls himself by no other title but Peter "an apostle of Jesus Christ," by which it is manifest, that we are not Peter's, but Peter is ours. Again, when Paul came to Antioch, he withstood Peter to his face, because he was to be blamed; which he would not have done if Peter had possessed any supreme authority or could not have lied, as they say. But, as I have said thereupon, Paul, seeing the dissimulation of Peter, said unto him, "If thou, being a Jew, livest after the manner of Gentiles, and not as do the Jews, why compellest thou the Gentiles to live as do the Jews? We who are Jews by nature, and not sinners of the Gentiles, knowing that a man is not justified by the works of the law, but by the faith of Jesus Christ, even we have believed in Jesus Christ, that we might be justified by the faith of Christ, and not by the works of the law" (Gal. 2:14-16).

Let us then see how it is possible that Peter should be chief apostle; for if he was principal, who loved Christ the best, it is evident that St. John would be the chiefest of the apostles, for Christ appointed him to take care of His mother (Jn. 19:26), and John lay in the bosom of Jesus, whilst he supped (Jn. 12:23).

Can a Lawful Council be Called by a Pope Seeking Election

But to the matter in hand. I ask, whether a lawful council can be called but by the pope? To which, I am sure, the papists will answer negatively. Then I ask, if the pope can call a Council before his election? To which I know they will reply, he cannot. If then no council is lawful without a pope, and that none who is laboring to be elected pope can assemble a council, then the council which confirms the pope as superior over the church, is not lawful; because it was not convocated by a pope, there being then none elected.

But, being thus driven from that argument, they fly to another, and say, that Christ commanded Peter to feed His sheep: but He commanded all the rest to do the same, saying, "Go ye therefore and teach all nations, baptizing them in My name" (Matt. 28:19). But the pope does not obey the commandment of Jesus Christ; for he doth not feed the sheep, but devours them, like a roaring lion who walks about to seek his prey. Now I wish the pope would obey the commandment which God gave unto St. Peter. For I should not regret his having authority to preach Christ to all the world, but he leaves the preaching of the gospel, and usurps the authority of being Head of the Church, which of right belongs to none but Christ.

The Pope Transgresses the Commands of God

It is true the pope is primate of the Church, but it is not the divine or catholic church, but the diabolical one; for he transgresses the commandments given in general to St. Peter and the rest of the apostles. For when Christ sent his twelve disciples to preach the gospel of repentance and the kingdom of God, He said, "Behold, I send you forth as sheep, amongst wolves": but the bishop of Rome is like a wolf amongst sheep, eating and devouring the poor sheep of Christ; and when they are hid by fear, he takes the voice of a sheep to betray and devour them. He excuses himself from preaching upon its being too low and mean an office for him, saying, he hath lower officers and ministers for that work; whilst he is taken up with seeing and attending to the singing of the masses. But I answer to the first, that if the office of preaching was not below St. Peter, who had received all his authority and power from Christ Himself, methinks those who call themselves the successors of Peter, should not esteem the preaching of the gospel too mean for them.

Qualifications for a Bishop or Elder

St. Paul writes to Timothy what "every bishop ought to be; A bishop, saith he, must be blameless, the husband of one wife, sober, of good behaviour, given to hospitality, apt to teach, not given to wine, no striker, not given to filthy lucre, but one that ruleth well his own house, having his children in subjection with all gravity" (1 Tim. 3:1-4). Now let us arraign the pope before St. Paul, and examine whether by Paul's rule he be guilty or not.

The first command to a bishop is to be blameless; but we have proved that the bishop of Rome transgresses all the commandments of God, by which he stands guilty. The second is, that he be the husband of one wife, in which the bishop of Rome errs mightily; for he allows concubines, and counts filthiness better than lawful and honest marriage. The third is, that he should be sober, and full of wisdom and virtue, which the bishop of Rome very little observes. The fourth is, that he be liberal, given to hospitality, not greedy of filthy lucre; but the bishop of Rome is full of avarice and oppression. The fifth is, that he be apt to teach; but our diabolical "father" accounts maintaining the glory of God by preaching, as too mean an office for him; notwithstanding his predecessor Peter either preached the gospel, or sinned against God in not observing that commandment, "Go ye, and preach the gospel over all the world."

But he will imprison, slay, and burn those who do preach the Word, and would himself be their executioner, if he did not find others to do it in his stead; by which we may see that he loves himself more than he loves God. What shall I say more? He disobeys the orders of St. Paul: give verdict therefore whether he be guilty or innocent.

Feeding the Sheep

But now we will proceed to their other arguments, and first, to their maintaining Peter to be the chief, for which they allege his being commanded to feed the sheep. To which I answer, that all the apostles were commanded as well as he, to feed the sheep of Christ, in these words of the gospel, "Go ye unto all and preach," etc. for the preaching of the gospel signifies nothing else but feeding His sheep. And their other argument is not more substantial, when they say Peter was a fisher of men; for I say, Andrew and John were, by the same authority, made fishers of men: for fishers of men are really nothing but preachers of Christ.

Now, if the preaching of the gospel be unlawful without authority from Peter or the pope, then the preaching of St. Paul was not lawful, because he did not receive his authority from Peter; notwithstanding the pope accounts himself a God, saying, I cannot lie; therefore I have spoken truth. To which I answer, that if he be not greater than Peter, he may lie; for Peter denied Christ thrice, Peter then lied thrice: and St. Paul afterwards reproved him for his dissimulation.

But the bishop of Rome lies notoriously, if in nothing else, but in his pretending to be the head of the Christian church, and having the keys of heaven. For, if the pope has the keys of heaven, I make this query, When the pope is dead, and none hath the keys, how can any soul enter into heaven? No person till he be elected pope having the keys; whence it must follow, that the pope being dead, Heaven's gates are closed! But it is a folly to say, that the pope hath the keys of heaven and hell, when Christ is our only Mediator, our Gate, Head, Shepherd, Redeemer, and Sovereign Lord; who after he had taught, instructed, done many miracles, and suffered death, for us, and pronounced salvation to all that believe on his name, and from the power of his passion faithfully believe to be saved, ascended into heaven with great honour and glory, and is seated on the right hand of God His Father, where He intercedes for us; remaining for ever with His blessed Father, and the Holy Ghost, one God in Trinity, and three Persons in unity, full of power and virtue, and free from vice and sin; remaining with us by His Spirit, and being in every respect equal with His Father, till He shall come in glory to be Judge of all the world: whose goodness is inscrutable, mercy inexpressible and glory most inestimable. He is our Governor and Master. He is our Shepherd and Redeemer, and we are His subjects and sheep; we are ransomed by His blood and washed by the waters of baptism to show that we are His sheep; none else is our pastor or Lord; neither the pope, nor any on earth, can be our head; else we should become a monster having two heads. Paul writing to the Corinthians, says, that all is ours; Peter, Apollos, and all the other apostles were ours, and we are Christ's and Christ is God's; whereby it appears that Peter is not a head, but a minister unto us. Therefore, we must esteem God our spiritual Father, who, by the passion of Christ, took for all who believe in Him, all the pains of death and hell. He gave us the spirit of adoption, "whereby we cry, Abba, Father" (Rom. 8:15).

The Pope is Not Our Spiritual Father

If the pope then will be called our spiritual father, we shall have three fathers, whereof the one is carnal, and two spiritual: neither can the pope be so, for Christ is the immaculate Lamb, and only Son of God, endued with all power. On the other hand, the pope is an unclean and ravenous wolf, and only son of the devil his father, from whom he hath received his authority and office.

But I would fain know, whether the pope be our spiritual, carnal, or diabolical father? In the first place, I see not how he can be our carnal father, because he lives celibate, and makes a profession of chastity. Neither can he be our spiritual father, being so addicted to the world and worldliness; then it follows that he must be our diabolical father! Let us therefore conclude, that as it was said of Christ, "Thou art My Son, this day have I begotten Thee." God will say to the pope, "Thou art My enemy, this day have I destroyed thee." And as Christ was of the order of Melchisedek, so the pope is of the order diabolic. But as Christianity is spiritually very good, and well designed; yet if there be not good order to preserve it, it must decay. As the body of a man could not be healthy with two heads, four arms or four feet; so these Christian countries could never well subsist under the distraction of two equal sovereigns.

One Sovereign Who Ordains Kings and Rulers

But some may question me then, and say, What then, you would not have any kings or emperors? But to that I answer, that God, who sent His only Son down into the world, made Him King over it, putting all spiritual and temporal authority into His hands; He by His sovereignty hath placed kings to be his lieutenants over the earth; but He hath not ordained any supreme bishop: for we find none so authorized by the holy Scripture. Now, if the papists say, that the pope is heir to Him, I would advise him then to stay [wait] till Christ were [is] dead before they seized upon His kingdom; because no heirs take the possession of their inheritances, till after the death of their predecessors.

Christ Alone is Our Shepherd

Moreover, the papists say, that as under the old law there was a high priest or archbishop of the Jews, so there ought now to be a head or supreme minister amongst Christians. To which I answer, that the priesthood of Aaron and Moses represented the supremacy of our Saviour Christ, not the pope. For Christ, who came down to the earth, and suffered death for us, says of Himself, that He was our Messias, and that he was the true Bread which came down from heaven and our only Shepherd. For St. John testifies that He says, "I am the door; he that entereth not by Me into the sheepfold, but climbeth up some other way, is a thief; but he that entereth in by the door is the

Shepherd of the sheep. To him the porter openeth; and the sheep hear his voice: and he calleth his own sheep by name, and leadeth them out and the sheep follow him, for they know his voice; and a stranger will they not follow" (Jn. 10:1-5). But the pope, not coming by Christ, is a thief. Therefore all true and good sheep ought to fly from him: for he comes to devour, not feed them; to prey upon them, not instruct them.

Christ's Kingdom is Not of This World

But the papists, being thus scourged with their own rod, that is, with their own argument, say further, that after the disciples had preached about the cities, after they returned to Jesus, He asked them, whether they had any sword with them? and that they answered, "Here are two swords" (Lu. 22:38). Now they urge further, that one of the swords signifies the spiritual, the other the temporal power; which reason, as shall be showed hereafter, is foolish and vain. For first we ought to consider from whence the apostles came. They had been sent to preach Christ to all people, and to show the light to those that sat in darkness. Secondly, we must consider the power Christ had on earth; for He said Himself, that His kingdom was not of this world; and there are two sorts of authority, the one spiritual, the other temporal. On which account St. Paul writes in his first epistle to the Corinthians, As the body is one, and hath many members, for several uses; so there are also in the church of Christ, amongst the spiritual ministers; first apostles; secondly prophets; thirdly teachers; and some temporal ministers, as kings, emperors, governors, and lieutenants. Now Christ was a spiritual minister, as He testifies of Himself, saying, "My kingdom is not of this world." And again, when two brethren came unto Him and requested Him to divide their inheritance between them, He answered "Man, who made Me a judge, or a divider over you?" (Lu. 2:14). The third thing to be considered, is, that Christ spoke to the disciples concerning the swords ironically. Fourthly, that all the apostles answered together, "Behold, here are two swords." Fifthly, you may observe in the text, that the apostles understood not what Christ meant.

By all which we may easily understand that text; for after the apostles had been sent to preach the gospel of truth, when they returned to Jesus, He said unto them, "Had you any sword with you then?" as much as to say, "When I sent you first out, you would have staves with you, but now what do you think, hath not My grace kept you from all evil?" Or else, "What need have you of a sword?" Then his disciples, not Peter only, not understanding what Christ said, answered, "here are two swords" (Luke 22:38).

By which we see Christ spoke ironically, and that all the disciples made answer, not Peter alone; as if Peter should say, I have two swords, the one signifying my temporal authority, and the other signifying my spiritual jurisdiction: neither would nor could Christ give a temporal authority, forasmuch as He was a spiritual minister.

Editorial note: Verse 38 was curiously perverted in the famous Bull of Pope Boniface VIII (1235-1303) "Unam Sanctum" to prove his possession of both secular and spiritual authority. This stands on the level with that which finds the relations of the Church and State foreshadowed in the "two great lights" of Genesis 1:16. In the paragraphs above the king is trying to make clear that Christ did not give Peter the authority indicated by one sword (to rule in temporal matters) and another sword (to rule in spiritual matters). He emphasizes the fact that Peter alone did not say, "Here are two swords," (Luke 22:38), but as we see in the text, "all" said it not just Peter. The king rightfully observes that the disciples did not understand what our Lord was trying to convey to them and were "spinning their wheels" on a subject which the Lord was not discussing at all.

Who Spoke First

And the papists err extremely in one argument, where they say, that Cephas is a head, whereas in truth, Cephas is a stone; but when these their arguments are weakened, then they cry it is probable, that Peter was the chief apostle, because he spake first at that time, concerning our dispute, and so answered in behalf of all the apostles.

But it is more likely Peter was not the prince over the rest, for St. Paul says, "For I suppose I was not a whit behind the very chiefest apostles" (2 Cor. 11:5). "For in nothing I am behind the very chiefest apostles" (2 Cor. 12:11), in which number Peter is included. Now, we must not dispute what is most *probably* true, but what is most *certainly* true. Nevertheless, let us examine whether it be probable or not; for Andrew sometimes spake first, and it is not to be doubted but that each of the apostles sometimes spoke first; but it does not therefore follow, that he who speaks first, must be bishop of the bishops. His first speaking at that time, may signify that he was of a very courageous spirit; or else that he could have desired to have been the greatest. But Christ said, "They that humble themselves like a little child, shall be the greatest in the kingdom of heaven," neither is there any lofty proud title in the kingdom or church of Christ, as you may see in that magnificate in Luke 1, for God loves humility, and Christ says, in Mark, "If any man desire to be first, the same shall be last of all and servant unto all" (9:35). And in another evangelist He saith, "Whoso receiveth one such little child in My name, receiveth Me, and unless ye become as little children, ye shall not be fit for the kingdom of heaven" (Matt. 18:3-5).

Popes Assume Great Titles and Power

Nor does Peter attribute so high a title to himself, as the pope takes upon him. For he writes thus in his epistle, "Peter a servant and an apostle of Jesus Christ," and no more.

But the pope, what does he say? "Paul the third, by the grace of God, the most holy pope and father, deputy to Peter, and vicar to Christ, king of kings, prince of princes, bishop of bishops, and God on earth!" Behold therefore, how he calls himself God, and blasphemes Christ. Behold how he is filled and puffed up with pride and vanity. Behold how large and fair a name and title he takes, though he be a venomous serpent; calling himself the most Holy Father, whereas he is a detestable thief, and contaminated with all uncleanness. He calls himself the pope, which word signifies, father unto all nations, whilst he brings them to destruction. Nay, he calls himself the vicar of Christ, and deputy of St. Peter, and God upon earth; whilst he is vicar to Beelzabub, deputy to Lucifer, and a terrestial demon; for he would seem to be very good, whilst he is very wicked. And it is no wonder if the ministers of the devil appear brave and triumphant outwardly, for St. Paul writes to the Corinthians, "No marvel that false apostles and deceitful workers can transform themselves," Satan himself being "transformed into an angel of light."

Wherefore you may easily discern the true minister of the word from the false Antichrists; because the true apostles walk after the Spirit of God, and the false walk after the flesh. Let us therefore see whether the pope be the minister of God, or the devil: which I fear he will prove; proclaiming himself a good man, a most holy bishop, a king of kings: whereas he is the tyrant of tyrants. All others exercise their tyranny over bodies, but this wolf and tyrant exercises his tyranny over the souls of men, constraining the poor simple lambs of God to forsake their faith, whereby they are saved, to follow his abominable traditions and diabolical precepts; which if they refuse to obey, to wit, adoring images, and offering to his idols and devils, he burns, racks, and torments them, or forces them to a costly recantation.

Those Who Exalt Themselves Shall Fall

During the reign of my late father (King Henry VIII), when the pope's name was blotted out of our books, he stopped the mouths of Christians with his six articles, as if he would choke them. And at this day in France, before any one is burnt, a little before the execution, they cut out his tongue that he may not speak.

Considering then that the pope is the minister of Lucifer, I am in good hopes, that as Lucifer fell from heaven into hell, so the pope his vicar will fall from the great glory of his papacy, into contemptible derision.

For David hath said in his Psalms, "With the pure Thou wilt show Thyself pure, and with the froward Thou wilt show Thyself froward" (18:26). Again, the pope hath taken God's honour away from Him; therefore I hope God will divest him of his honours and glory. As the virgin Mary saith, "He hath put down the mighty from their seats, and exalted them of low degree" (Lu. 1:52). Take heed of thyself then, O pope, for if thou tumblest, thou wilt have a terrible fall. As a man who is got up into a high tower, would have a huge leap if he should fall down; so thou who hast exalted thyself into the heavens, wouldest fall down in to the abyss of hell: as Christ foretold of Tyre and Sidon.

Jesus Christ is Our Supreme Potentate

But to return to the pope's primacy. I know very well that the Scripture speaks of one God, one faith, one baptism, but no mention of one pope. Now, if Peter had been a God on earth, and vicar of Christ, we should have been baptized into his name. But Paul, who affirms himself to be inferior to none of the other apostles, will not allow us to be baptized in his name. Nay, he is so far from having us baptized in the name of Peter, that he will not have it said, I am of Peter, or of Paul, or of Apollos. And now that the papists cannot prove by the Scriptures that we ought to have one pope, they run to similitudes; saying, that as creatures in the earth, as the bees, have a king over them, so all Christians ought to have one king and pope. To which I will answer three ways: First, that their reason is not extracted from the holy Scripture, but from their own invention. Secondly, that all the bees which are in the world, or in christendom, have not a king. Thirdly, that if all bees have their king, so have we, namely, Jesus Christ.

But the papists will then say, that if we condemn the papacy, we shall condemn our forefathers as heretics. I will answer to that, as God answered Elijah, when he said to the Lord that the children of Israel had forsaken his covenant, and were unjust and wicked, "Yet I have left Me seven thousand in Israel, all the knees which have not bowed to Baal" (1 Kings 19:18).

Old Customs May Be Polluted

Neither must we imagine, but that there have been many Christians in the world, some of whom have spoken openly against the papacy, and others that have kept their knowledge and sentiments to themselves; but the papists will not suffer us to know more than our fathers. But I know very well, that our religion consists not of old customs, or the usage of our fathers; *but in the holy Scriptures, and the divine word;* and that (if you think antiquity and custom makes a thing good) is older than the world: for God is the Word, who is without beginning, and shall continue without end; and if you think truth ought to be followed and obeyed, all truth is contained in that book, [the Bible]. Our religion ought not to be steered or governed by our forefathers; for Ezekiel saith, "Walk ye not in the statutes of your fathers, for they were polluted" (20:18). Moreover, our God and Saviour, and Redeemer, Jesus Christ said, "I am the way, and the truth, and the life" (Jn. 14:1). He did not say, I am the old custom.

The papists then say, that though Christ did not indeed ordain the pope, yet he left it to the church to do it. To which I ask, how Peter then was elected the universal bishop? For all things necessary to our salvation are written in the Bible, as St. Paul testifies in his epistle to Timothy, where he says, "But continue thou in the things which thou hast learned . . . And that from a child thou hast known the holy Scriptures, which are able to make thee wise unto salvation, through faith which is in Christ Jesus" (2 Tim. 3:14, 15).

Pope By Divine Right?

But to what purpose do we go about to prove that Peter is not the head of the church? For [even if we] allow [that] he had been so, that does not conclude that the bishop of Rome is the principal head: for the papists themselves cannot prove that Peter was ever at Rome. By the Scripture they cannot prove it; nor by an true history; therefore the bishop of Rome loses one of his great titles, *Papa ex jure divino*, (pope by divine right,) for no authority can be ex jure divino, unless it be confirmed by the Scripture.

Well then, we have him in a great plunge, since he must be forced to say, Paul, pope by human traditions; for if he be not bishop by the divine word, but only by human traditions, then all kings, princes, and other magistrates, may abrogate the statutes and institutions made by their fathers, as we have seen before.

If every one then had known this, the pope had been poor long ago. Now the papists say, that the bishop of Rome was instituted by the primitive church; but no more so than Mahomet, for they began near the same time. The first pope was Gregory the Great. He was elected in 590 A. D. when all manner of wicked errors were advanced in Christendom.

Clementine Epistles are False

Nevertheless, to prove that Peter was at Rome, they produce the *Clementine* epistles, but we will prove them counterfeited, and falsified by the papists. For in them it is written that Peter was at Rome, in the second year of the reign of *Claudius*, and lived there twenty-five years.

171

But Christ was crucified in the eighteenth year of *Tiberius*, who reigned five years after the crucifixion: *Caius Caligula* reigned four years; and Claudius two; which makes it eleven years before supposedly Peter went to Rome: but in the eighteenth year of our Lord, Paul found St. Peter in Jerusalem (Gal. 1:18), thus we see their history is false. And it cannot be true that Clement wrote those epistles unto James, for James was dead before Clement was bishop.

Moreover, St. Peter was the leader among the Jews, and not the Gentiles. St. Paul glories in several places that he was the apostle of the Gentiles. Again, St. Paul, writing to the Galatians, says, that he went up to Jerusalem to see Peter. Therefore it is most probable that Peter dwelt for the most part in Jerusalem, or in the adjacent cities. And here we may see the craft of the devil, and the power of God. For notwithstanding the devil, to establish his power, invented the Clementine epistles; though they were counterfeited by the papists, yet I say, God by His goodness and clemency towards His elect, hath caused the said epistles to be so written, that every one who hath read history, may plainly comprehend and understand, that they were feigned by serpentine subtilty, and by some abominable and obdurate papists.

In several other instances also, we may discover their false subtilty; for notwithstanding that the holy Scripture saith, Idols are senseless things, and without life; they have often framed images, which sometimes rolled their eyes, sometimes turned their heads, sometimes moved their hands, and sometimes their whole bodies: by which means they made people believe, that an image, made of wood, heard and understood them; all of it being made so [true] to life, that, as they turned them, they made the head and eyes of the image to turn also. But, as Daniel with ashes or sand proved that the idol Bel did not eat, but his priests, so by the holy Scriptures, the confession of several persons, and by observation and experience, they have been proved to have been mere machines, and other instruments.

Early Church Fathers
Disapproved the Idea of a Pope

Since we see that Peter neither was the chief, nor was at Rome; considering that they say the pope cannot lie, we will examine whether they themselves have not acknowledged that no person ought to be the primate of the church.

For Gregory the first hath written, that none ought to be pope. Gregory was then bishop of Rome, and Maurice was emperor, and there were many heresies in Christendom; and the bishop and patriarch of Constantinople at that time pretended to be the universal bishop, who was much favoured by Maurice; but *Gregory declared then in his writings, that there ought to be no principal in the church.*

And now the papists are overthrown by this; they say that by the consent of the general councils and doctors, a universal bishop was established under the name of pope: whereas for four or five hundred years after Christ, there was no person in the world that was distinguished or called by that name. Moreover, when there were several contentions about the papacy, all learned persons detested the opinion that there must be a pope: and sometimes the very bishops of Rome themselves abhorred it. And St. Cyprian writing concerning the unity of the church, saith, "There is one bishop, of whom every bishop holds a share. For as there are many beams in the sun, yet the light is but one: many branches in a tree, several streams from a fountain; in like manner the church is but one; which being illuminated by the brightness of our Lord, who extends His beams throughout the world, yet nevertheless the clarity [light] is but one, namely Jesus Christ." Likewise the same *Cyprian*, being bishop of Carthage, calls the bishop of Rome his companion. Moreover, St. Jerome, bishop of Rome, (ep. ad Evag.) humbles the style of primate; saying, If there be any question of the authority of a primate of the church, also there are bishops of nations and cities, it follows not therefore that there is a primate over all the world, for the world is much greater than any city. And also in the *council of Carthage* it was decreed, that none should be called the first or primate of the bishops.

What shall I say more? It was consented and agreed by all, for almost six hundred years after Christ, that none ought to be pope. (August. Epist. 28 ad Const.) How could Peter then have been primate, or the pope his successor? For Peter in his epistles does not command, but prays and beseeches the ministers of God. Likewise, when he is accused for having communicated with the Gentiles, he does not burn his accusers, as the pope does his: but excuses himself, and shows a submission.

Again, when he was sent to Samaria by his brethren and companions, he readily obeyed their decree, and went down to that city.

Interpretation of Daniel, Chapter Seven

Of this detestable and diabolical pope, the holy Scriptures, in several places, give us a plenary demonstration; some of which I shall show unto you. As first, in the seventh of Daniel, it is set down how that Daniel, who was beloved by Belshazzar, saw a vision, which appeared to him thus; I saw, says Daniel, in my vision by night, and behold, the four winds of the heaven strove upon the great sea, and four great beasts came up out of the earth. The first was like a lion, and had eagle's wings; and I beheld till the wings thereof were plucked, and a man's heart was given to it. The second beast was like unto a bear, and it raised up itself on one side; and they said thus unto it, Arise, devour much flesh. The third was like unto a leopard, which had upon the back of it four wings of a fowl, and the said beast had also four heads. After this I beheld the fourth beast, which was dreadful and terrible, and strong exceedingly; and it had great iron teeth, and devoured every thing, and it had ten horns. And behold, there came up among them another little horn, before whom there were three of the first horns plucked up by the roots; and it had eyes, and a mouth speaking blasphemies. And I beheld till I saw the Ancient of Days did sit, and I beheld, saith Daniel, till the judgment was set for the horn, and till the beast was slain, and his body given to the burning flame: and it shall be for a time, times, and a half.

Now the four winds, and the four beasts, as *Melancthon, Oecolampadius,* and all learned writers say, signify the four monarchies; the first was that of the

Assyrians, whereof Nebuchadnezzar was emperor, who, after he had been made like unto the beasts for a long season, had the understanding of a man given him again.

The second signified the empire of the Persians, which was a dominion of great cruelty.

The third notified the Grecian empire, which was immediately raised to its grandeur; and the four wings and four heads signify the four emperors which succeeded *Alexander,* and divided amongst them the Grecian monarchy; for *Seleucus* was made king of Syria, *Ptolemy* got Egypt, *Antigonus* Asia, and *Cassander* Greece.

The fourth beast signifies the terrible monarchy of the Romans, out of which arises a little horn, which is antichrist; and antichrist hath two eyes, namely, the pope and *Mahomet;* for notwithstanding that the pope doth not speak against Christ, as Mahomet doth, nevertheless I answer, that the pope is as much, or rather more, an antichrist than Mahomet. For as he who flatters us is our enemy, though he seems to be our friend; so the pope, who styles himself the servant of the servants of God, is the enemy of Christ; whilst under the shadow of religion, he puts in practice all hypocrisy, idolatry, dissimulation, and all sort of traditions.

His time shall be a time, times, and a half; that is to say, his days shall be shortened, for the number of seven stands for a perfect number in Scripture; for St. Paul says, the just fall seven times a day, that is, often. Now the half of seven is three and a half; therefore we must interpret by that imperfect time, that those days shall be shortened.

Interpretation of
2 Thessalonians 2:1-7 and 1 Tim. 4:1-3

St. Paul also, in two epistles, prophesies of the pope; first, writing to the Thessalonians, he says, "Now we beseech you, brethren, by the coming of our Lord, that ye be not soon shaken in mind, or be troubled, neither by spirit, nor by word, nor by letter, as that the day of Christ is at hand. Let no man deceive you by any means, for that day shall not come, except there come a falling away first, and that man of sin be revealed, the son of perdition; who opposeth and exalteth himself above God, so that he as God sitteth in the temple of God, showing himself as God. And now ye know what withholdeth, that he might be revealed in his time. For the mystery of iniquity doth already work; only he who now letteth, will let until he be taken out of the way." Again, St. Paul, writing to Timothy, speaks thus: "Now the Spirit speaketh expressly, that in the latter times some shall depart from the faith; giving heed to doctrines of devils, speaking lies in hypocrisy, forbidding to marry, and commanding to abstain from meats, which God hath created to be received with thanksgiving of them which believe." Now let every one be asked, if the pope hath not forbidden certain meats, at certain times, and they must all confess he hath, for most folks have felt it; or, perchance, I should not be a liar if I said, that almost all folks have felt it.

And concerning the prohibition of marriage, ask their own priests. St. Peter tells us, that there shall come in the last days scoffers, etc.

Interpretation of Rev. 17:3-5 and 2 Tim 3:1, 2

St. John, in the Apocalypse, says, Seven angels poured out the vials of God's wrath upon the earth; (Rev. 15:1) and the signification is probable to be thus—The first vial to be the Assyrian monarchy, when the people of Israel became captive to Nebuchadnezzar. The second the Persian monarchy. The third vial the monarchy of the Grecians, which Alexander first established. The fourth was the Roman monarchy, which the apocalypse, because of its grandeur, says, the fourth vial was poured upon the sun. The fifth is our antichrist the pope. The sixth vial is the dominion of Mahomet. The seventh vial signifies the end of the world, and the day of judgment.

In the following chapter he declares, that one of the seven angels came and talked with him, and showed him the state, honour, and riches of the pope: for he says, "he saw a woman sit upon the beast, full of names of blasphemy, having seven heads and ten horns; and the woman was arrayed in purple, and scarlet colour, and decked with gold; having a golden cup in her hand, full of abominations, and filthiness of her fornications: and upon her forehead was written, Babylon the mother of harlots, and abominations of the earth, Rev. 17:3-5. The seven heads signify the seven hills which antichrist dwells on; for Rome is built upon seven mountains. The seven horns are the number of the kings who made war with the Lamb, and the Lamb overcame them, for he is Lord of lords, and King of kings; then another angel came down from heaven, crying, Babylon is fallen, and is become the habitation of devils. Thence I hope, that the kingdom of antichrist shall be destroyed: for though the wicked may prosper for a

178

time, their dominion shall not last; but those who study the law of the Lord, their prosperity shall last for ever. St. Paul, writing to Timothy, says, "This know also, that in the last days, men shall be lovers of their own selves, covetous, boasters, proud, blasphemers, etc. 2 Tim. 3:1, 2. And the prophet Isaiah saith, that Christ shall smite the earth, with the rod of his mouth, and with the breath of his lips shall he slay the wicked, Isaiah 11:4.

Since we see then that the reign of antichrist shall not last for ever, we must wait for the destruction of Babylon, and submit ourselves to the will of the Lord.

The Conclusion

In the first part of our book, we have proved and declared that Peter was not primate of the church, by confuting all the papistical reasons for it.

In the second, we have proved that they cannot produce and allege any true testimony, that St. Peter was at Rome.

In the third part, we have proved from themselves, that they have said they ought not to have the primacy.

In the fourth part, we have explained the prophecies speaking of antichrist. Since then the pope is that wicked one, very son of the devil, an antichrist, and an abominable tyrant, let us pray unto the Lord to preserve those still in the light who have seen it: and that he will show the sincere, pure, and true light unto those who sit in darkness: that all the world may glorify God in this life, and be partakers of the eternal kingdom of heaven in the world to come, by the merits of Jesus Christ our Saviour; to whom, with the Father, and the Holy Ghost, be all honour, glory, dominion, and praise, for ever and ever. Amen.

The Original Manuscript

The original manuscript of King Edward was written in French by the king's own hand, and was entitled "L'Encontre les abus du Monde,"—and means, Against the Abuses of the world. *Strype* has elaborated the import of the title as: Against the Abuses Imposed upon the Faith and Worship of Christians by the Pope, whom he calls Antichrist.

It is authenticated to be the king's own composition, by a note written at the end by his instructor in the French language. When translated, it reads as follows:

> *"Just as a good painter can represent*
> *the visage, look, countenance, and bulk*
> *of a prince; so by the writings, words,*
> *and actions of a prince, one may easily*
> *understand what spirit is in him, and*
> *to what he is addicted. As one may*
> *see by the writings of this young king,*
> *who composed and wrote this book,*
> *being not yet full twelve years old, and*
> *without the help of any person living;*
> *except as to the subject, which he had*
> *heard of many, and the remembrance*
> *which he had of books that he had read.*
> *For, from the time he began to write*
> *the said book and until he finished it,*
> *the said book was always in my keeping,*
> *even to the present time."*

Preface to
Prayers and Instruction on Prayer

The prayers in this section are alive with the Spirit of God breathing through them. They are personal, Bible-oriented and they throb with life. They are written as if they just poured out of a heart of a true believer kneeling next to you.

Take this as an example: "Forasmuch as nothing pleaseth Thee that is done without faith, [though it] appear before the blind world ever so beautiful and commendable, but it is counted in Thy sight sinful and worthy of condemnation: yea the self sin and condemnation. This is most humbly to desire Thee, O Father, for Christ's sake, to breathe into my heart by the Holy Spirit, this most precious and singular gift of faith, which worketh by charity [love]."

Do not read these prayers in a hurry. Take one of these prayers a day, perhaps, and meditate on it. List Scriptures that come to mind as you read it and yourself pray right there and then.

It is difficult for us even to imagine the ignorance of the people and the spiritual darkness that prevailed in England while the Roman Church held sway. Primers in the English language were not allowed. In the year 1519, six men and a woman were burned at Coventry because they were teaching their children to repeat the Lord's prayer and the ten commandments in the English language. The children were admonished sternly by the persecutors of Rome not to meddle again with the Lord's prayer the doctrines or the commandments in English if they wished to escape a similar fate. [1]

This was the last edition of the Primer in the reign of King Edward VI. It exhibits the principles which those who were then in authority desired to convey to every house and to inculcate in every heart throughout the land.

N. A. Woychuk

[1] William Byron Forbush, editor, *Foxe's Book of Martyrs*, John C. Winston Co., Philadelphia, 1926.

Section 3

Prayers
and Instruction on Prayer

Excerpts from Edward VI Primer

These were prepared by Archbishop Thomas Cranmer and Bishop Nicholas Ridley, with the participation and approval of King Edward VI.

Instructions on Prayer

Examine thine own conscience with what kind of temptation or sin thou art most encumbered withal; andpray earnestly to God for remedies thereto. Asking of Him all things needful both for soul and body; privately for thine own self and thy family, and generally for all the Christian congregation. "If any of you lack wisdom (that is, any gift of grace), let him ask of God, that giveth to all men liberally, and upbraideth not; and it shall be given him" (Jas. 1:5).

Upon consideration of thine own lack, and the common lack of the congregation, remember that God commandeth thee by prayer to call upon Him for remedy, aid, and help, saying: Ask, seek, knock; watch and pray; "call upon Me," saith God, "in the day of tribulation."

Consider that God doth not only command thee to

pray, but also promiseth graciously to hear and grant all thine honest, lawful, and godly requests and petitions; saying, "Ask, and ye shall have; knock, and it shall be opened unto you; every one that asketh, hath," etc. "Call upon me," saith God, "in the day of trouble, and I will deliver thee."

Thou must stedfastly believe God's promises; and trust undoubtedly, both that He can and will perform them. "Ask in faith," saith St. James, "nothing doubting"; for why shouldest thou doubt, seeing that the holy Scripture testifies of God, that He is faithful, just, and true in all His words and promises; saying, "The Lord is faithful in all His words. He will ever be mindful of His covenant. The truth of the Lord endureth for ever."

Thou must ask of God all thy petitions and requests, for His mercy and truth sake; for Christ Jesus' sake, and in His blessed and holy name. "Save me, O God," saith David, "for Thy name's sake." "No man cometh unto the Father, but by Me," saith Christ. "Verily, verily, I say unto you, whatsoever you ask of the Father in My name, He will give it you." Mark, that He saith, "In My name." Thou must never ask for worldly and corruptible things, pertaining to this transitory life, such as bodily health, wealth, or strength, without employing in thy prayer such conditions as these, "If it be Thy will, O Lord; if it stand with Thine honour and glory; if it be for my soul's health, profit, and advantage; if not, Thy will be done and not mine." All these things your heavenly Father knoweth that ye have need of before ye ask of Him. With this condition prayed Christ, saying, "Father, if it be possible, let this cup pass from Me; nevertheless, not as I will, but as Thou wilt." With this condition prayed David for his return in his exile.

Thou must not appoint any certain time to God for granting thy requests; but utterly commit that to His godly will and pleasure, who knows best what time of granting thy requests is most commodious and profitable for thee.

Thou must in any wise take heed, when thou prayest, that thou art in love and charity with all men; or else, all these aforesaid things profit nothing at all. For, like as a surgeon cannot heal a wound perfectly, so long as any iron remains in it, even so, prayer cannot profit, so long as the mind is cankered and defiled with guile, fraud, deceit, rancour, hatred, malice, and such other like wretchedness; for brotherly reconciliation must needs go before prayer. As Christ saith, "If thou offerest thy gift at the altar, and there rememberest that thy brother hath aught against thee, leave there thine offering before the altar, and go thy way; first be reconciled to thy brother, and then come, and offer thy gift."

Prepare thyself therefore to prayer with the aforesaid considerations; and, being adorned and garnished with faith, hope, charity, meekness, soberness, equity, pity, and godliness, go in Christ's name, and pray unto God with all diligence.

And in thy faithful prayers remember that thou pray for our sovereign.

Miscellaneous Prayers

The eyes of all look up and trust in Thee, O Lord, Thou givest them meat in due season. Thou openest Thine hand,

185

and fillest with Thy blessing every living thing. Good Lord, bless us, and all Thy gifts which we receive of Thy bounteous liberality, through Christ our Lord. Amen.

The King of eternal glory make us partakers of His heavenly table. Amen.

❈

Blessed is God in all His gifts; and holy in all Hisworks. Our help is in the name of the Lord, who hath made both heaven and earth. Blessed by the name of our Lord, from henceforth, world without end.

Most mighty Lord and merciful Father, we yield Thee hearty thanks for our bodily sustenance, requiring also, most entirely, Thy gracious goodness, so to feed us with the food of Thy heavenly grace, that we may worthily glorify Thy holy name in this life, and afterwards be made partakers of the life everlasting, through our Lord Jesus Christ. Amen. Lord save Thy church, our king and realm; and send us peace in Christ. Amen.

❈

All ye whom God hath here refreshed with this sufficient repast, remember your poor and needy brethren; of whom some lie in the streets, sore, sick, naked, and cold; some are hungry and so dry, that they would be glad of the least draught of your drink, and of the smallest paring of your bread. They are your own flesh, and brethren in Christ; bought as dearly with His precious blood as you were; but yet our Lord has dealt more easily with you than with them, and more austerely with them than with you; relieve them therefore according to your power; and give to God all glory, honour and praise, for ever and ever. Amen.

❈

A Comprehensive Prayer

O gracious Lord, and most merciful Father, who hast, from the beginning of mine age, hitherto delivered me from innumerable perils and dangers, both of soul andbody; I most heartily thank Thee. And yet, forasmuch as I feel in myself so many faults and imperfections, such readiness to evil, and such frowardness and slackness to do good, I quake and tremble for fear of Thy fierce wrath, and strict judgment. But when I consider with myself, that Thou commandest me by prayer to crave of Thee all things necessary for soul and body, I conceive a little hope of recovery of that which I standin need of. And it fully comforteth me, and maketh me not a little joyful, when I remember, that Thou, O Father, not only commandest me to pray, but also, of Thine exceeding great mercy, promisest graciously to hear my lamentable suit; and mercifully to grant to me my lawful and needful requests.

My faith, confidence, and sure trust is, that Thou art true and just in all Thy words and promises, and both canst and will perform them, and grant me mine honest petitions. Howbeit, for all that, I will not presume to ask them in mine own name, neither for mine own merit nor deserving; but for Christ Jesus' sake; and in His blessed and holy name; and for Thy mercy and truth's sake.

But, touching all those things that pertain to this my corruptible body and transitory life, I humbly beseech Thy fatherly goodness to grant me them, so far as they agree unto Thy holy will, pleasure, honour and glory, and may be best suited to my improvement, profit and advantage. Nevertheless, I beseech Thee, good Lord, grant me them, not at such time as I fancy to be best; but at such time, as shall appear most meet to Thy godly Majesty, unto whose protection I fully and wholly commit both me and all mine.

Moreover, seeing that Thou regardest no prayer, unless it be made in love and charity, I humbly beseech Thy gracious goodness, that I may always pray in charity, make my petitions and requests in charity, use Thy gracious gifts and benefits in charity, and lead all my whole life and conversation in charity.

And, finally, I heartily pray Thee, that I may daily, through the assistance of Thy Holy Spirit, more and more mortify all my carnal desires and sinful affections. And vouchsafe to prosper both me and mine, and all the Christian congregation, in all our honest and godly affairs: increase also Thy gracious gifts in us; and confirm us and establish us so in grace, that we may go forward in all goodness; grant this most merciful Father for Jesus Christ's sake, our only Mediator and Advocate. So be it.

❀

Almighty and most merciful Father, I have erred and strayed from Thy ways like a lost sheep. I have followed too much the devices and desires of my own heart. I have offended against Thy holy laws. I have left undone those things which I ought to have done; and I have done those things which I ought not to have done; and there is no health in me. But Thou, O Lord, have mercy upon me a miserable offender. Spare Thou me, O

God, which confess my faults, restore Thou me, that am penitent; according to Thy promises, declared unto mankind in Christ Jesus our Lord. And grant, O most merciful Father, for His sake, that I may hereafter live a godly, righteous, and sober life, to the glory of Thy holy name. Amen.

Almighty God, the Father of our Lord Jesus Christ, which desirest not the death of a sinner, but rather that he may turn from his wickedness, and live; and hast given power and commandment to Thy minister, to declare and pronounce to Thy people, being penitent, the absolution and remission of their sins; and pardonest and absolvest all them which truly repent, and unfeignedly believe Thy gospel; I beseech Thee to grant me true repentance and Thy Holy Spirit; that those things may please Thee which I do at this present, and that the rest of my life hereafter may be pure and holy; so that at the last I may come to Thy eternal joy through Jesus Christ our Lord. Amen.

❊

Albeit whatsoever is born of flesh is flesh, and all that we receive of our natural parents is earth, dust, ashes and corruption; so that no child of Adam hath any cause to boast himself of his birth and blood, begotten in sin, conceived in uncleanness, and born by nature the children of wrath; yet, forasmuch as some for wisdom, godliness, virtue, valour, eloquence, learning and policy, are advanced above the common sort of people, unto dignities and temporal promotions, as men worthy to have the superiority in a Christian commonwealth; and,by this means, have obtained among the people a more noble and worthy name: we most entirely beseech Thee, from whom cometh the true nobility to so many as are born of Thee, and are made Thy sons through faith, whether they are rich or poor, noble or simple, to give a good spirit to our superiors; that, as they are called gentlemen in name, so they may show themselves in all their doings, gentle, courteous, loving, merciful and liberal unto their inferiors, living among them as natural fathers among their children; not oppressing them, but favouring, helping and cherishing them: not destroyers, but fathers of the commonalty; not enemies to the poor, but aiders, helpers and comforters of them—that when Thou shalt call them from this vale of wretchedness, they, having first shown gentleness to the common people, may receive gentleness again at Thy merciful hand, even everlasting life; through Jesus Christ our Lord. Amen.

As the bird is born to fly, so is man born to labour; for Thou, O Lord, hast commanded in Thy holy word, that man shall eat his bread in the labour of his hands, and in the sweat of his face: yea, Thou hast given commandment, that if any man will not labour, the same should not eat; Thou requirest of us, also, that we withdraw ourselves from every brother that walketh disorderly, and giveth not his mind unto labour; so that Thy godly pleasure is that no man be idle, but every man labour according to his vocation and calling. We most humbly beseech Thee to engrave in the hearts of labourers and workmen a willing disposition to travail for their living, according to Thy word; and to bless the labourer's pains, and travails of all such as either till the earth, or exercise of other handicraft; that they, studying to be quiet, and to meddle with their own business, and to work with their own hands, and through Thy blessing enjoying the fruits of their labours, may acknowledge Thee, the giver of all good things, and glorify Thy holy name. Amen.

�֎

Albeit, Lord, Thou art the giver of all good things, and through Thy blessing men become rich, that are godly and justly rich; yet we are taught in Thy divine Scriptures, that riches, and the cares of worldly things smother and choke up Thy holy word: and that it is more easy for a camel to go through the eye of a needle, than for a rich man to enter into the kingdom of heaven. Again, that they which will be rich, fall into temptations and snares, and into many foolish and noisome lusts, which whelm men into perdition and destruction, (for covetousness is the root of all evil,) we, therefore, perceiving by Thy blessed word so many incommodities, yea pestilences of man's salvation to accompany riches, most entirely beseech Thee to bless such as Thou hast made rich, with a good, humble, loving, and free mind.

Let them remember themselves to be Thy dispensers and stewards, may they not set their minds upon the deceitful treasures of this world, which are more brittle than glass, and more vain than smoke, nor yet heap up thick clay against themselves; but liberally and cheerfully bestow part of such goods, as Thou hast committed unto them, upon their poor neighbours; make for themselves friends of this wicked mammon; be merciful to the needy; be rich in good works; and ready to give and to distribute to the necessity of the saints, laying up in store for themselves a good foundation, against the time to come; that they may obtain everlasting life, through Jesus Christ,

Thy Son, our Lord. Amen.

❊

As riches, so likewise poverty is Thy gift, O Lord; and as Thou hast made some rich to despise the worldly goods, so hast Thou appointed some to be poor, that they may receive Thy benefits at the rich man's hands. And as the godly rich are well beloved of Thee, so in like manner are the poor, that bear the cross of poverty patiently and thankfully; for good and evil, life and death, poverty and riches, are of Thee, O Lord; we therefore most humbly pray Thee, to give a good spirit to all such as it hath pleased Thee to burden with the yoke of pov erty; that they may, with a patient and thankful heart, walk in their state, like to that poor Lazarus of whom we read in the gospel of Thy well-beloved Son, who chose rather patiently and godly to die, than unjustly or by force to get any man's goods, and by no means envy, murmur, or grudge against such as it hath pleased Thee to endue with more abundance of worldly goods: but knowing their state, although ever so humble and base, to be of Thee their Lord God, and that Thou wilt not forsake them in this their great need, but send them things necessary for their poor life, may continually praise Thee, and hope for better things in the world to come; through Jesus Christ our Lord. Amen.

❊

O heavenly Father, all we that unfeignedly profess Thy holy religion, and faithfully call on Thy blessed name, are Thy sons, and heirs of everlasting glory: yet, as all the members of a body have not one office, so likewise we, being many, and making one body, whereof Thy dearly beloved Son is the head, have not all one gift, neither are all called to one office, but as it hath pleased Thee to distribute, so receive we. We therefore most humbly pray Thee to send Thy Spirit of love and concord among us; that, without any disorder or debate, every one of us may be content with our calling; quietly live in the same; study to do good unto all men, by the true diligent exercise thereof, without too much seeking of our own private gain; and so order our life, in all points, according to Thy godly will, that by well doing we may stop the mouths of such foolish and ignorant people as report us to be evil doers; and cause them, through our good works, to glorify Thee our Lord God in the day of visitation. Amen.

❁

Most merciful Father, grant me to covet with an ardent mind those things which may please Thee; to search them wisely, to know them truly and to fulfil them perfectly, to the laud and glory of Thy name. Order my living so that I may do that which Thou requirest of me; and give me grace that I may know it, and have will and power to do it; that I may obtain those things which are most convenient for my soul.

Gracious Lord, make my way sure and straight to Thee, so that I fall not between prosperity and adversity; but that in prosperous things I may give Thee thanks, and in adversity be patient, so that I be not lift up with the one, nor oppressed with the other. And that I may rejoice in nothing but that which moveth me to Thee; nor be sorry for anything but for those things which draw me from Thee; desiring to please nobody, nor fearing to please any besides Thee.Most loving Father, let all worldly things be vile unto me, for Thee; and be Thou my most special comfort above all. Let me not be merry with the joy that is without Thee; and let me desire nothing besides Thee; let all labour delight me which is for Thee; and let all the rest weary me which is not in Thee. Make me to lift up my heart oftentimes to Thee; and when I fall, make me to think on Thee and be sorry, with a stedfast purpose of amendment.

Loving Lord, make me humble, without feigning; cheerful, without lightness; sad without mistrust; sober, without heaviness; true, without doubleness; fearing Thee, without desperation; trusting in Thee, without presumption; telling my neighbours their faults meekly, without dissimulation; teaching them with words and examples, without any mockings; obedient without arguing; patient without grudging; and pure without corruption.

Give me also, I beseech Thee, a watchful spirit, that no curious thought withdraw me from Thee. Let it be so strong, that no filthy affection draw me backwards; so stable, that no tribulation break it. Grant me also to know Thee; diligent to seek a godly conversation; to please, and finally hope to embrace Thee, for the precious blood sake of that immaculate Lamb, our only Saviour Jesus Christ, to whom, with Thee, O Father, and the Holy Ghost, three Persons and one God, be all honour and glory, world without end. Amen.

Specific Prayers

Prayer for the Work of the Holy Ghost

So frail is our nature; so vile is our flesh; so sinful is our heart; so corrupt are our affections; so wicked are all our thoughts, even from our childhood upwards, that of ourselves we can neither think, breathe, speak, or do any thing that is praiseworthy in Thy sight. O heavenly Father; yea, except Thou dost assist us with Thy merciful goodness, all things are so far out of frame in us, that we see nothing present in ourselves but Thy heavy displeasure and eternal condemnation. Vouchsafe, therefore, O loving Father, to send Thy Holy Spirit unto us, which may make us new creatures; put away from us all fleshly lusts; fill our hearts with new affections and spiritual motions; and so, altogether renew us both in body and soul, through His godly inspiration, that we may die unto the old Adam, and live unto Thee in newness of life, serving Thee our Lord God in holiness and righteousness all the days of our life. Amen.

For the True Knowledge of Ourselves

It is written in Thy holy Gospel, most loving Saviour, that Thou camest into this world, not to call the righteous, that is, such as justify themselves, but sinners unto repentance. Let me not therefore, O Lord, be in the number of those who boasting their own righteousness, their own works and merits, despise that righteousness which cometh by faith, which alone is allowable before Thee. Give me grace to acknowledge mine own self as I am, even the son of wrath by nature, a wretched sinner, and an unprofitable servant; and wholly to depend on Thy

195

merciful goodness with a strong and unshaken faith; that in this world Thou mayest continually call me unto true repentance, seeing I continually sin, and, in the world to come, bring me unto everlasting glory. Amen.

For a Pure and Clean Heart

The heart of many naturally is corrupt and unsearchable through the multitude of sins, which lie buried in it, insomuch that no man is able to say, My heart is clean, and I am clear from sin. Remove from me, therefore, O heavenly Father, my corrupt, sinful, stony, stubborn, and unfaithful heart. Create in me a clean heart, free from all noisome and ungodly thoughts. Breathe into my heart by Thy Holy Spirit, godly and spiritual motions; that out of the good treasure of the heart, I may bring forth good things, unto the praise and glory of Thy name. Amen.

For a Quiet Conscience

The wicked are like a raging sea, which is never in quiet; neither is there any peace to the ungodly: but such as love Thy law, O Lord, they have plenty of peace; they have quiet minds and contented consciences, which is the greatest treasure under the sun; given of Thee to so many as seek it at Thy hand, with true faith and continual prayer. Give me, O Lord, that joyful jewel, even a quiet mind and a contented conscience; that I, being free from the malicious accusations of Satan, from the crafty persuasions of the world, from the subtle enticements of the flesh, from the heavy curse of the law, and fully persuaded of Thy merciful goodness toward me, through faith in Thy Son Jesus Christ, may quietly serve Thee, both bodily and spiritually, in holiness and righteousness all the days of my life. Amen.

For Faith

Forasmuch as nothing pleaseth Thee that is done without faith, though it appears before the blind world ever so beautiful and commendable, but it is counted in Thy sight sinful and worthy of condemnation. This is most humbly to desire Thee, O Father, for Christ's sake, to breathe into my heart by Thy Holy Spirit, this most precious and singular gift of faith, which worketh by love. Whereby also we are justified, and received into Thy favour; that I, truly believing in Thee, and fully persuaded of the truth of Thy holy word, may be made Thy son, and inheritor of everlasting glory, through Jesus Christ our Lord. Amen.

For Love

Thy cognizance and badge whereby Thy disciples are known, O Lord and Saviour Jesus Christ, is love, which cometh out of a pure heart, a good conscience, and of faith unfeigned. I pray Thee, therefore, give me this Christian love and perfect charity, that I may love Thee my Lord God, with all my heart, with all my mind, with all my soul, and with all my strength; doing always out of love that only which is pleasant in Thy sight. Again, that I may love my neighbour and Christian brother as myself; wishing as well to him as to myself; and ready at all times to do for him whatsoever lieth in my power, that when we shall all stand before Thy dreadful judging place, I, being known by Thy badge, may be numbered among Thy disciples, and so, through Thy mercy, receive the reward of eternal glory. Amen.

For Patience

When Thou didst live in this world, O Lord Christ, Thou didst show Thyself a true mirror of perfect patience, suffering, quietly, not only the venomous words, but also cruel deeds of Thy most cruel enemies; forgiving them, and praying for them which most despitefully handled Thee. Give me grace, O most meek and loving Lamb of God, to follow this Thy patience; quietly to bear the slanderous words of mine adversaries; patiently to suffer the cruel deeds of mine enemies; to forgive them; to pray for them; yea, to do good to them; and by no means to go about once to avenge myself, but rather to give place unto wrath, seeing that vengeance is Thine, and Thou wilt reward: seeing also, that Thou helpest them to their right that suffer wrong; that I, thus patiently suffering all evils, may afterwards dwell with Thee in glory. Amen.

For Humility

What have we, O heavenly Father, that we have not received? Every good gift, and every perfect gift, is from above, and cometh down from Thee, which art the Father of lights. Seeing then all that we have is Thine, whether it pertain to the body or the soul, how can we be proud and boast ourselves of that which is none of our own? Seeing also, that as to give, so to take away, Thou are able; and wilt whensoever Thy gifts are abused, and Thou not acknowledged to be the Giver of them. Take, therefore, away from me all pride and haughtiness of mind; graft in me true humility, that I may acknowledge Thee the Giver of all good things, be thankful unto Thee for them, and use them unto Thy glory, and the profit of my neighbour. Grant also, that all my glory and rejoice may be in no earthly creatures, but in Thee alone, which doest mercy, equity and righteousness upon earth. To Thee alone be all glory. Amen.

For Mercifulness

Thy dearly beloved Son in His holy gospel exhorteth us to be merciful, even as Thou our heavenly Father, art merciful, and promised that if we be merciful to others, we shall obtain mercy of Thee, who art the Father of mercies and God of all consolation. Grant, therefore, that forasmuch as Thou art our Father, and we Thy children, we may resemble Thee in all our life and conversation; and that, as Thou art beneficial and liberal not only to the good, but also to the evil, so we likewise may show ourselves merciful, gentle and liberal to so many as have need of our help; that at the dreadful day of doom we may be found in the number of those merciful, whom Thou shalt appoint by Thy only begotten Son to go into everlasting life; to whom with Thee and the Holy Ghost be all honour and praise. Amen.

For True Godliness

In Thy law, O Thou Maker of heaven and earth, Thou hast appointed us a way to walk in, and hast commanded that we should turn neither on the right hand nor on the left, but do according to Thy good will and pleasure, without adding of our own good intents and fleshly imaginations. As Thou hast commanded, so give me grace, good Lord, to do. Let me neither follow my own will, nor the fancies of other men, neither let me be beguiled with the mask of old customs, long usages, fathers' decrees, ancient laws, nor anything that fighteth with Thy holy ordinances and blessed commandment but faithfully believe, and stedfastly confess that to be the true godliness, which is learned in Thy Holy Bible: and according unto that, to order my life unto the praise of Thy holy name. Amen.

For the True Understanding of God's Word

O Lord, as Thou alone art the Author of the holy Scriptures, so likewise can no man, although he be ever so wise, politic, and learned, understand them, except he be taught by Thy Holy Spirit, who alone is the school-master to lead the faithful unto all truth. Vouchsafe, therefore, I most humbly beseech Thee, to breathe into my heart Thy blessed Spirit, who may renew the senses of my mind, open my mind, reveal unto me the true understanding of Thy holy mysteries, and plant in me such a certain and infallible knowledge of Thy truth, that no subtle persuasion of man's wisdom may pluck me from Thy truth; but that as I have learned the true understanding of Thy blessed will, so I may remain in the same continually, come life, come death; unto the glory of Thy blessed name. Amen.

For a Life Agreeable to Our Knowledge

As I have prayed unto Thee, O heavenly Father, to be taught the true understanding of Thy blessed word, by Thy Holy Spirit, so I most entirely beseech Thee, to give me grace to lead a life agreeable to my knowledge. Suffer me not to be of the number of those, who profess that they know God with their mouth, but deny Him with their deeds. Let me not be like unto that son who said unto his father that he would labour in his vineyard, and yet laboured nothing at all, but went abroad loitering idly. Make me rather like unto that good and fruitful land, which yieldeth again her seed with great increase; that men seeing my good works, may glorify Thee, my heavenly Father. Amen.

For a Good Name

Nothing becometh the professor of Thy name better, O heavenly Father, than so to behave himself according to his profession, that he may be well reported of them that are of the household of faith. Yea, such sincerity and pureness of life ought to be in those who profess Thy holy name, that the very adversaries of Thy truth should be ashamed once to mutter against them.

Give me grace, therefore, I most entirely desire Thee, so to frame my life according to the rule of Thy blessed word, that I may give no occasion to speak evil of me; but rather so live in my vocation, that I may be an example to others to live godly and virtuously, unto the honour and praise of Thy glorious name. Amen.

For a Competent Living

Although I doubt not of Thy fatherly provision for this my poor and needy life, yet forasmuch as Thou hast both commanded and taught me by Thy dear Son to pray unto Thee for things necessary for this my life; I am bold at this present to come unto Thy divine Majesty, most humbly beseeching Thee, that as Thou hast given me life, so Thou wilt give me meat and drink to sustain the same. Again, as Thou has given me a body, so Thou wilt give clothes to cover it; that I, having sufficient for my living, may the more freely, and with the quieter mind, apply myself unto Thy service and honour. Amen.

For a Patient and Thankful Heart in Sickness

Whom Thou lovest, O Lord, him dost Thou chasten, yea every son that Thou receivest, Thou scourgest, and in so doing Thou offerest Thyself unto him, as a father unto his son. For what son is he whom the father chasteneth not? Grant, therefore, I most heartily pray Thee, that whensoever Thou layest Thy cross on me, and visitest me with Thy loving scourge of sickness, I may by no means strive against Thy fatherly pleasure; but patiently and thankfully abide Thy chastisement, ever being persuaded, that it is for the health both of my body and soul; and that by this means Thou workest my salvation; subduest the flesh unto the spirit; and makest me a new creature; that I may, hereafter, serve Thee more freely, and continue in Thy fear unto my life's end. Amen.

Bibliography

Cannon, John and Ralph Griffiths, *The Oxford Illustrated History of the British Monarchy,* Oxford University Press, Oxford, 1988

Chalmers, Thomas, *Sermons and Discourses,* Robert Carter & Brothers, New York, 1881

Chapman, Hester W., *The Last Tudor King - A Study of Edward VI,* Ulverscroft, Leicester, 1958

Douglas, J. D., *The New International Dictionary of the Christian Church,* Zondervan Publishing House, Grand Rapids, MI

d'Aubigne, J. H. Merle, *The Reformation in England,* Vol. 1, Banner of Truth Trust, London, 1962

Edward VI, *Seven Original Letters to Barnaby Fitzpatrick,* Strawberry-Hill, 1772

Forbush, William Byron, Editor, *Foxe's Book of Martyrs,* The John C. Winston Co., Philadelphia, 1926

Gorham, G. C., *Gleanings of a Few Scattered Ears, During the Period of the Reformation in England,* Bell and Daldy, London

Jackson, S. M., Editor-in-chief, *The Schaff-Herzog Encyclopedia of Religious Knowledge,* 15 Vol., Baker House, Grand Rapids, MI

Jordan, W. K., Editor, *The Chronicle and Political Papers of King Edward VI,* Cornell University Press, Ithaca, NY

Jordan, W. K., *Edward VI: The Young King,* Harvard University Press, Cambridge, MA, 1968

Loach, Jennifer, *Edward VI,* Yale University Press, New Haven, 1999

Lockyer, Herbert, *The Man Who Changed the World,* 2 Vol., Zondervan Publishing House, Grand Rapids, MI

Luke, Mary M., *A Crown for Elizabeth,* Coward-McCann Inc., New York, 1970

Luke, Mary, *The Nine Days Queen - A portrait of Lady Jane Grey*, William Morrow and Co., Inc., New York, NY, 1986

Macaulay, Thomas Babington, *Miscellaneous Essays and Poems,* T. Y. Crowell, New York

MacCulloch, Diarmaid, *The Boy King, Edward VI and the Protestant Reformation,* Palgrave Publishers, New York, 2001

Morrison, N. Brysson, *King's Quiver - The last three Tudors,* St. Martin's Press, New York, 1972

Newman, Albert H., *A Manual of Church History,* 2 Vol., The American Baptist Publication Society, Chicago

Pollard, A. F., *England under Protector Somerset - an Essay,* Russell & Russell, New York, 1966

Routh, C. R. N., *They Saw it Happen*, Basil Blackwell, Oxford, 1956

Ryle, John Charles, *Light from Old Times,* Chas. J. Thynne, London, 1890

Slocum, Stephen E., *Romanism in the Light of the Bible,* Tract Club of America, Chicago

Smith, H. Maynard, *Henry VIII and the Reformation*, Russell & Russell, Inc., New York

Weir, Alison, *The Children of Henry VIII*, (formerly entitled: *Children of England*), Ballantine Books, New York, 1996

_____ *Encyclopedia Britannica,* 15th Edition, Vol. 3, The University of Chicago, Chicago,1974

_____ *Historical Tales for Young Protestants,* Wycliffe Press, (The Protestant Truth Society), London

_____ *John Wicliffe, The Morning Star of the Reformation,* SMF Press, St. Louis

_____ *A Short History of the Reformation,* Wycliffe Press, (The Protestant Truth Society), London

_____ *Writings of Edward the Sixth Including Some Account of His Life,* Religious Tract Society, London, 1831

Index on the Biography

French Revolution 140
Fitzalan, Henry 44

Gage, Sir John 44
Galileo 140
Gardiner, Stephen, Bishop of Winchester 48, 56
Gospel 5, 16, 19, 27, 76, 77, 103, 117, 130-132
Grey, Lady Jane 23, 66, 67, 108, 119-122
Grey, Katherine 120
Guise, Mary, Queen Dowager of Scotland 57, 58, 70

Handel, George Frideric 139
Henry VIII, King of England 1, 9, 11, 12-15, 17, 19, 34, 44-46, 49, 56, 57, 71-73, 88, 128, 129
Herbert, Sir William 45
Hooper, John, Bishop of Gloucester 18, 33, 112
Hunter, William 122-125
Huss, John 8

Ironside, Harry A. 134-136

James I, King of England 137 *also* James VI, King of Scotland 137
James V, King of Scotland 57
Josiah, King of Judah 3, 41, 42, 113, 114, 116, 137

Knox, John 3, 5, 58, 59, 108

Laski, Jan 102
Latin Vulgate Bible 16
Latimer, Hugh, Bishop of Worchester 3, 53, 54, 60-62, 66, 126-128
Lever, Thomas 69, 70
Luther, Martin 5, 30, 100, 113, 132, 136

Macaulay, Lord 138, 139

Mallet, Dr. 95
Martyr, Peter 3, 100-102, 104
Melancthon, Philip 103
Michaelangelo 140
Milton, John 139
Montague, Sir Edward 45, 109, 110
More, Thomas 27-30

Newton, Isaac 140
North, Sir Edward 45
Northumberland - *see John Dudley*

Ochino, Bernardino 101, 102
Owens, Dr. 109

Paget, Sir William 44, 45, 48, 81
Palearion 107
Parr, Katherine, (sixth queen of Henry VIII) 13, 23, 49, 51, 57, 58, 70, 88, 89
Parr, William, Earl of Essex 44
Paulet, Lord William 44
Peckham, Sir Edmond 45
Petrarch 140
Petre, Sir William 45
Pickering, Sir William (Edward's ambassador to France) 67, 68
Pope Leo VIII 134
Pope Paul III 39
Pope Pius V 129
Pope of Rome 11
Poulain, Valerand 103
Primacy of the Pope - *see Against the Primacy of the Pope*
Privy Council 11, 25, 44-46, 50-52, 56, 58, 64, 66, 71, 73, 78, 80-85, 90-92, 94-96, 102, 117
Protector - *see Edward Seymour*
Protestant Reformation 1, 2, 5, 8, 19, 24, 31, 47, 48, 56, 57, 59, 62, 66, 78, 99, 101, 102, 112, 126,

Scripture Index